Antique Crazy Quilts and Their Stitches

Heather Hagan Bessler

Dedication

This book is dedicated to the ladies of several generations ago who created these beautiful quilts and embroidered them with loving care.

Acknowledgments

I wish to express my appreciation to the Porter County Museum and its Executive Director Kevin Pazour and Collections Manager Rachel Hulslander for their assistance. Special thanks to my son, Tom Bessler, for computer assistance.

Library of Congress Control Number: 2017902335

63 Roses Publishing
Valparaiso, Indiana

First Edition

ISBN-13: 978-0692846605
ISBN-10: 0692846603

Printed at Charleston, S.C. USA

Table of Contents

Porter County Museum, Valparaiso, Indiana

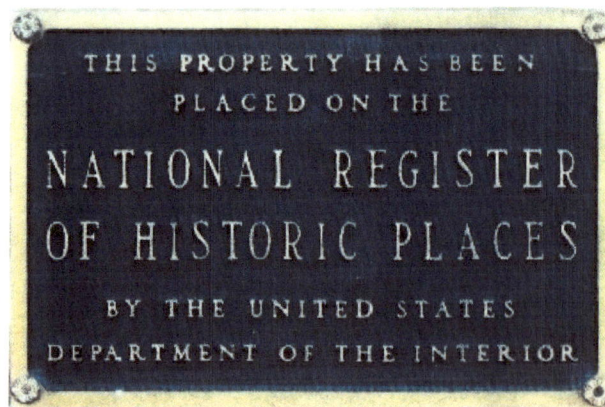

THIS PROPERTY HAS BEEN
PLACED ON THE

NATIONAL REGISTER
OF HISTORIC PLACES

BY THE UNITED STATES
DEPARTMENT OF THE INTERIOR

The Porter County Museum celebrated its 100th year in 2016. The Valparaiso facility is in the old jail that is on the National Register of Historic Places. In addition to quilts, there are many unique collections that illustrate the history and culture of Porter County.

Introduction

Hand embroidery and quilts have been in existence for hundreds of years although not always in the same project. It is amazing how many different quilt patterns can be made using little pieces of cloth. It is mind boggling how many different embroidery stitches can be made with a needle and thread one bite at a time. I tried hand embroidery when I was in grade school but quilting wasn't one of my activities until I joined the String-A-Long Quilt Guild. Books and magazines revealed a treasure trove of patterns and techniques. There among directions for log cabins and grandmother's flower garden were crazy quilts. They were something so different that I just had to make one --- and so it all started. You can't do justice to a crazy quilt with just one or two types of embroidery stitches. That meant some research in many books about hand embroidery, getting some embroidery thread, embroidery needles, and a hoop.   As the basics are mastered variations and combinations are simple to sew and of course more stitches lead to more crazy quilts!

When the quilt guild volunteered to help the Porter County Museum care for their quilt collection I was in the group. As the boxes were opened we saw log cabins, hexagons, grandmother's flower garden, and crazy quilts. I began taking photographs of various embroidered areas to see what stitches were used. Later when the pictures were developed I saw some stitches and combinations that were not familiar. It was like a gold miner discovering the mother lode! I felt that these quilts needed to be documented with more than written descriptions on paper. The museum's Executive Director, Kevin Pazour, agreed and allowed me full access to the quilts. More photographs and close study resulted in this book.

Crazy quilts are in a class of their own. The blocks are made with many fabric pieces of various sizes, shapes, and colors sewn randomly on a foundation. Antique crazy quilts may be embellished with appliqué, hand embroidery, buttons, beads, and ribbons but never have a repeating block pattern. Many questions, controversies, and surprises appear as the stories of this type of fascinating quilt unfold.

The first question asks why such small odd pieces are used in antique crazy quilts. The answer is simple. The patches are pieces left over from other projects such as dresses and shirts as well as good areas from worn out clothes. Nothing of use was wasted. Modern quilt makers have access to bolts of fabric but still cut small odd pieces because tradition says that is what makes these quilts unique.

Why are they called crazy quilts? There are several theories including the logic that the maker must be crazy to spend so much time and effort in sewing such small odd patches together. Then spend even more time hand embroidering and embellishing the blocks.   So it follows that a crazy quilter makes a crazy quilt. Another suggestion is the pattern of cracks in the crazed glaze of pottery is similar to the look of random patches of the quilts. As making these quilts became popular they became a fad that everyone had to try. Another word for fad is "craze" which very easily translated in to crazy and maybe the term "crazy quilt" was born.

Almost every crazy quilt has some hand embroidery on it. In antique crazy quilts the stitches are not just for embellishment, they are part of the construction. The surprising reason is that the patches were actually hand appliquéd to the foundation and the embroidery held down the loose edges. Modern crazy quilts are sewn with different methods so they don't have loose edges but the tradition of embroidering the seams and patches continues. Oops! Wait! There is a modern method called raw edge appliqué that has loose edges which are sewn down with regular stitching without folding them under. However a close inspection of antique quilts will reveal some raw edges under the lines of embroidery. This happened when the patch would not quite cover the foundation if the raw edge was folded under. So raw edges are not so modern after all!

Why are some quilts called Victorian crazy quilts? We have to go back to some historical events for this answer. When the industrial revolution occurred many people became wealthy. More money allowed aristocratic families to acquire large homes and many servants. Now the ladies didn't do household chores and had lots of leisure time. Embroidery was an acceptable activity for them. Time consuming fiber arts and expensive fabrics were ways to showcase their wealth. The greater the number of stitches the lady knew and the more elaborate the project projected the aura of greater wealth. Crazy quilts made of luxury fabrics like silk, velvet, and brocades embellished with hundreds of embroidery stitches became the signature of the upper classes. This was the time when Victoria was queen of England and her name was used to classify this type of ornamental crazy quilt. She reigned for over 63 years and her interests influenced all levels of society. Her one passion was to make collections of various things. So it was inevitable that her subjects would mimic this by gathering items like teacups, spoons and buttons as well as larger items. Gathering collections became so popular that a fad of having exactly 99 (no more/no less) objects became a goal. The embroidery on crazy quilts then became a "collection of 99" different stitches. For a more elaborate decorative look the 99 stitches were combined to make motifs and wider lines covering more of the fabric. The quilt was also a good way to show their 99 button collection. When this fad ended, crazy quilts still were covered with a glorious amount of colorful intricate embroidery. Now any crazy quilt with vast numbers of stitches layered, stacked, and mirrored is referred to as a Victorian style Crazy Quilt.

Controversies arise when serious opinions about quilts are expressed. Some quilters argue that crazy quilts are not quilts for two reasons. First they usually do not have batting so they do not have the required three layers to be a quilt. Loyal supporters maintain that there are three layers because most crazy quilt tops are made with the patches sewn to a foundation. Therefore, there is a top layer of patches, the foundation layer, and the backing. That adds up to three layers. The second objection is that it has to have quilting to be a quilt. Since crazy quilts are usually tied they can't be quilts. A rebuttal answers that the description of a quilt is that the layers are fastened together with stitches. Ties are stitches and tied quilts fit that requirement so crazy quilts are quilts. Arguments aside, I hope that we can agree that crazy quilts are unique and deserve the respect that their history demands. Besides this, crazy quilts are fun to look at and fun to make.

LeMoyne Star Crazy Quilt

A beautiful example of crazy patch, this quilt features seven LeMoyne Stars and two fans. The top is embellished with a magnificent variety of hand embroidered stitches and motifs. The fabrics include silk, velvet, cotton and brocade in many solid colors as well as some prints. The backing is machine seamed sateen fabric. Wool was used for the batting. The binding is ribbon attached by hand sewing.

The 15" blocks were pieced on a foundation. They are sewn in a straight set of three blocks in four rows. The quilt is sewn by hand and with a red border. The finished size is 63" long by 49" wide. It does not have a signature but was made about 1900. The quilt is in good condition.

Le Moyne Star Quilt Stitches

Arrow

Stacked Arrowhead

Two Color Arrowhead

2 Color Layered Blanket

Blanket

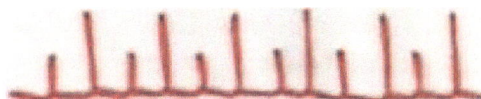

Long and Short Blanket

Chain

Detached Twisted Chain

Cross Stitch

Double Cross

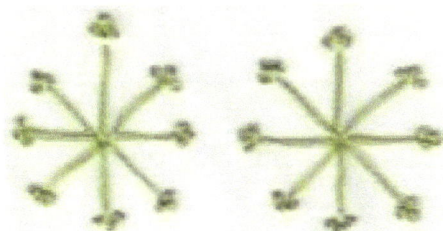

Eyelet and French Knots

1-2 Extended Feather

1-2 Simple Feather

1-3 Simple Feather

Closed Straight Feather

Double Feather

Le Moyne Star Quilt Stitches

Double Simple Feather

Extended Feather Layered

Mirrored Single Feather

Simple Feather

Straight Feather

Triple Simple Feather

Boxed Fly

French Knot

Double Straight Feather

Mirrored Double Feather

Alternating Single Feather

Single Feather

Triple Feather

Uneven Triple Simple Feather

Stacked Fly

Mirrored Herringbone and French Knot

Le Moyne Star Quilt Stitches

Shadow Herringbone

Stacked Holbein Stitch

Lazy Daisy Flower Chain

Straight Stitch Knot

Combinations

Arrowhead and Arrow

Stacked Arrow and Arrowhead

Y Stitch and Arrowhead

Y Stitch and Two Color Arrowhead

Blanket and Straight Stitch

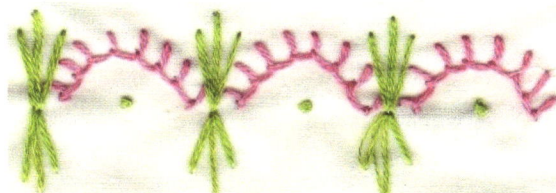

Sheaf, Blanket and French Knot

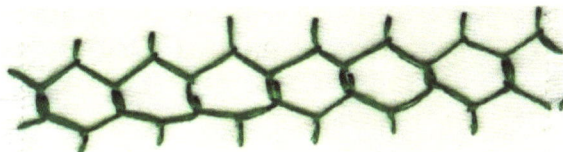

Mirrored Open Cretan

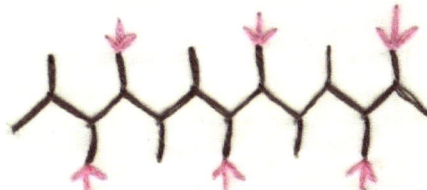

Open Cretan and Arrow

Le Moyne Star Quilt Stitches

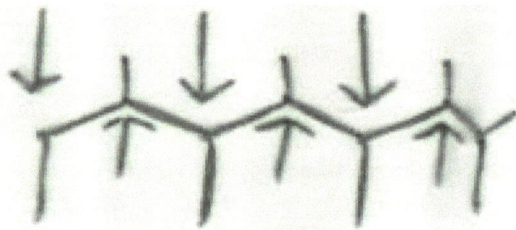

Open Cretan and Arrow

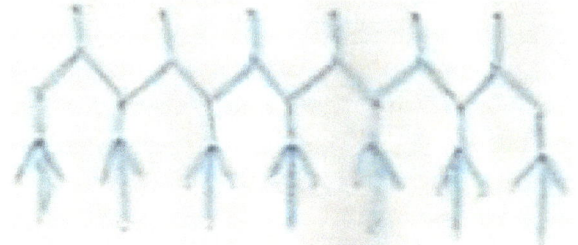

Open Cretan and Arrow

Cross Stitch and Arrow

Cross Stitch and Straight Stitch

Cross Stitch Line and
French Knot

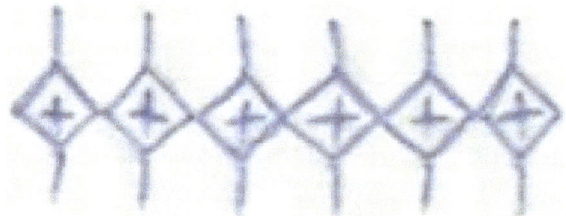

Mirrored Y Stitch and Cross

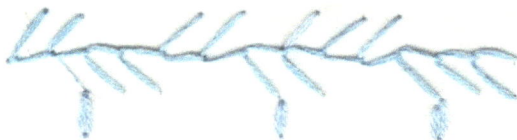

2-3 Simple Feather and
Lazy Daisy

Angled Double Single Feather,
Straight Stitch, and Couching

Cross Stitch and Feather

Single Feather and French Knot

Feather and Lazy Daisy

Feather and Lazy Daisy Fan

Le Moyne Star Quilt Stitches

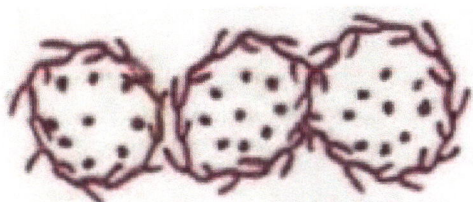

Feather Circles and French Knots

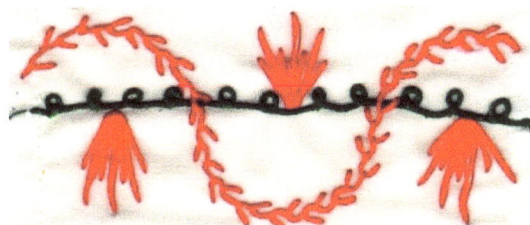

Feather, Loop and Uneven Fan

Piled Simple Feather and Lazy Daisy Fan

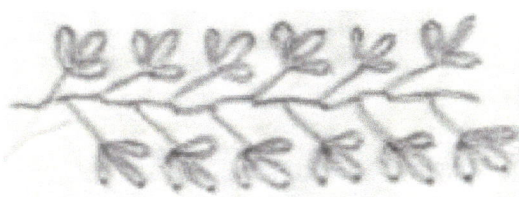

Simple Feather and Lazy Daisy Fans

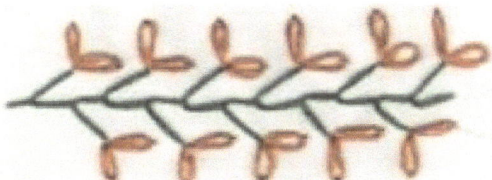

Simple Feather and Lazy Daisy

Simple Feather and Lazy Daisy

Single Feather and Lazy Daisy

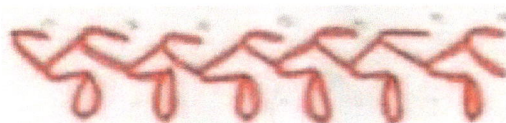

Straight Feather, Lazy Daisy and French Knot

Triple Feather and Lazy Daisy

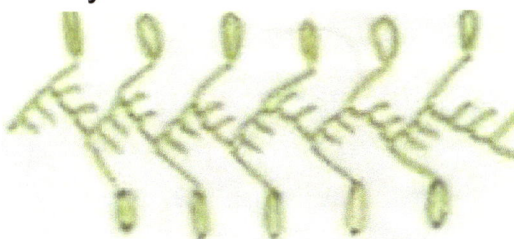

Uneven Triple Feather and Lazy Daisy

Le Moyne Star Quilt Stitches

Fly and Slipped Straight Stitch

Herringbone and Lazy Daisy

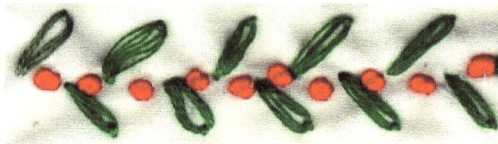

Lazy Daisy and French Knot

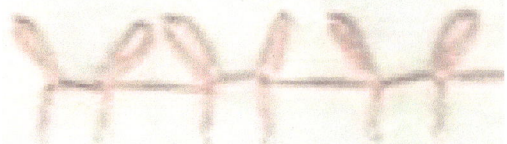

Nun's Stitch and Lazy Daisy

LeMoyne Star with Straight Feather and Lazy Daisy Stitches

Farmer's Day Crazy Quilt

An apron is one of many interesting appliqued details on this quilt which is embellished with embroidery stitches worked in various colors of yarn. The blocks are pieced on a foundation but are rectangles and free form shapes instead of the expected squares The fabrics include cotton, silk, velvet, wool, and brocade. The backing is seamed silk. There is no batting. The quilt is tied.

The quilt was sewn by hand with a finished size of 65 ½ " (length) by 58" (width). It is dated about 1914 with an appliqued ribbon dated 1914. There is no signature. There are several deteriorated areas.

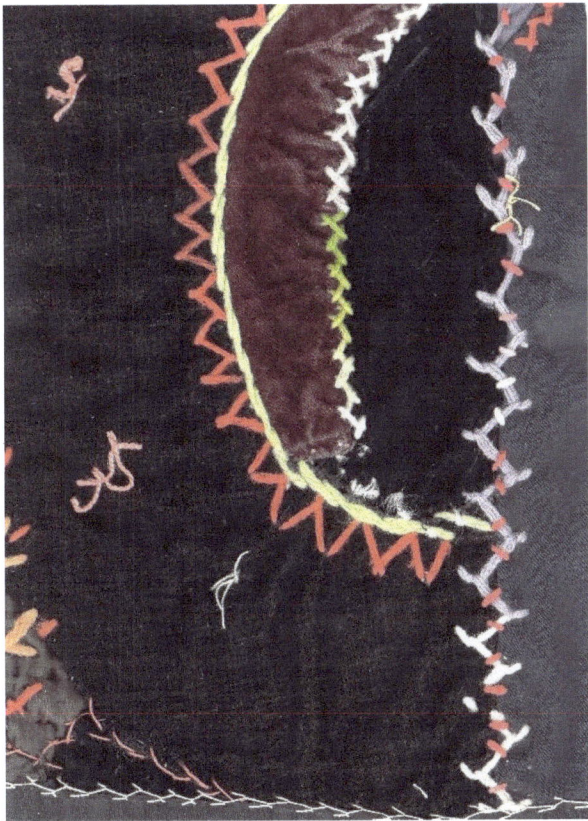

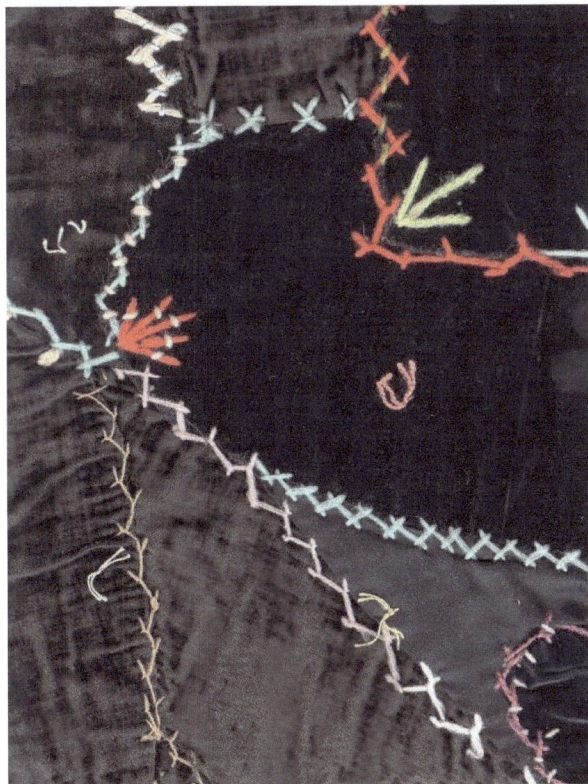

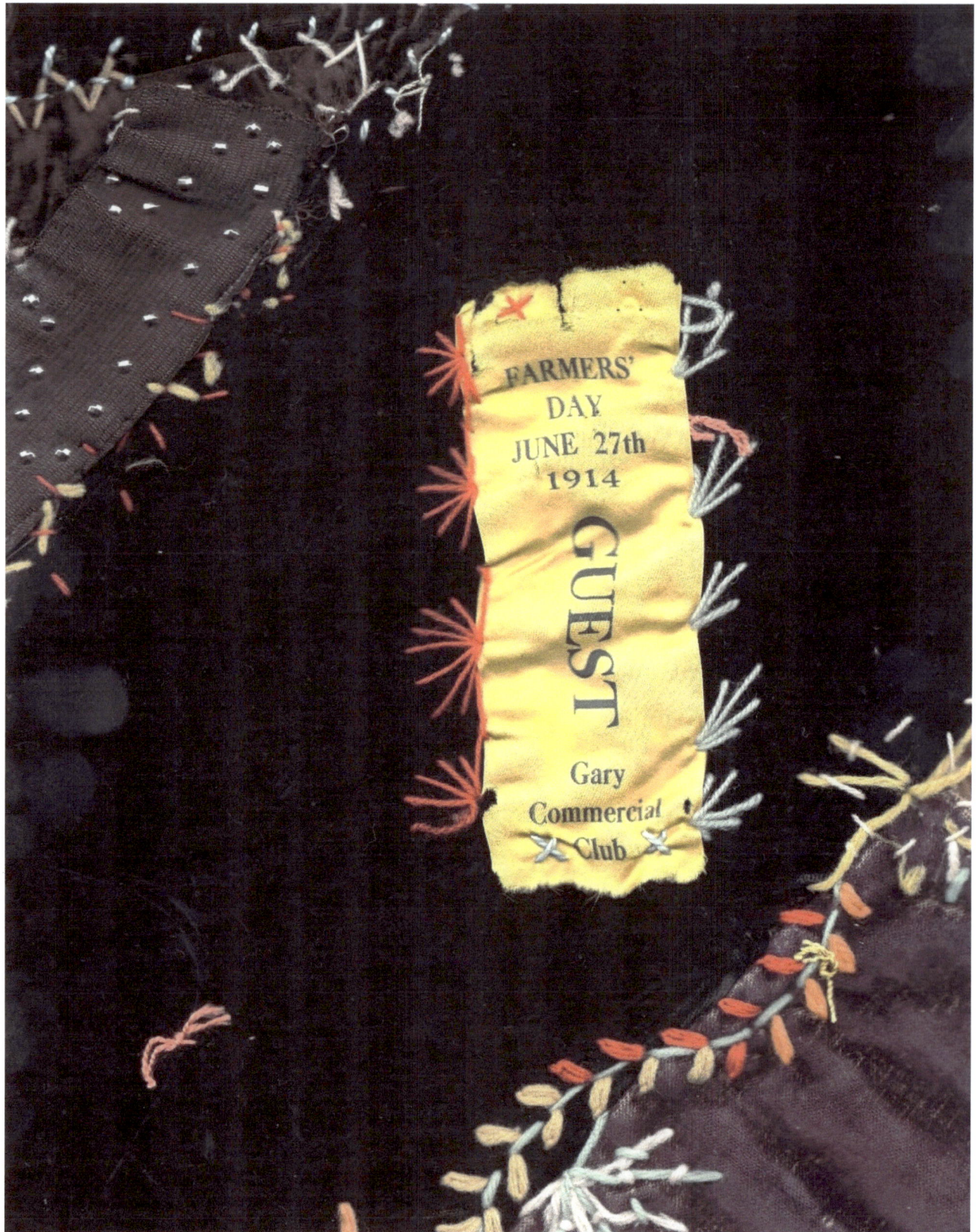

FARMERS'
DAY
JUNE 27th
1914
GUEST
Gary
Commercial
Club

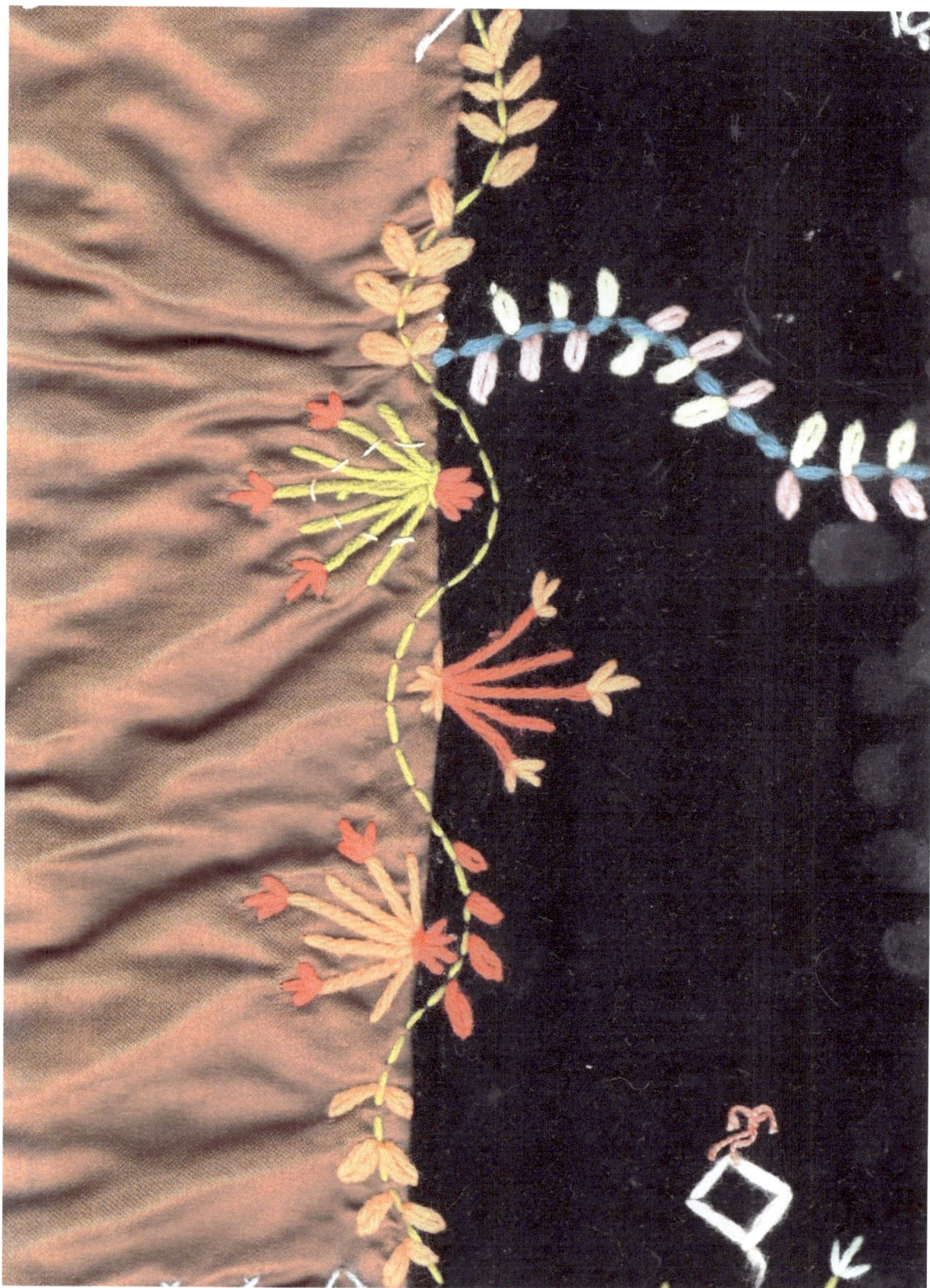

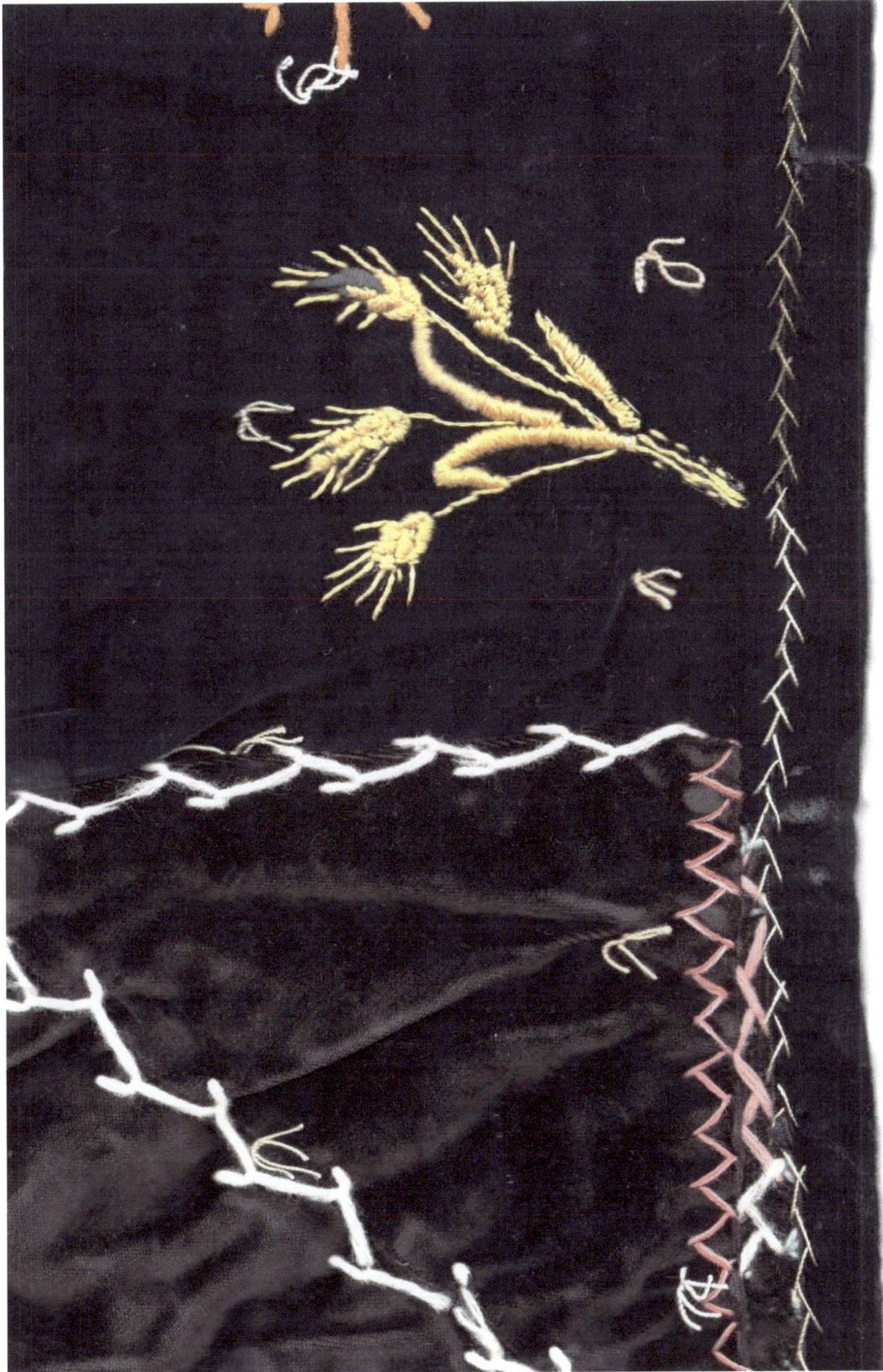

Farmer's Day Crazy Quilt Stitches

Arrow

Arrow

Arrow

Two Color Arrowhead

Arrowhead

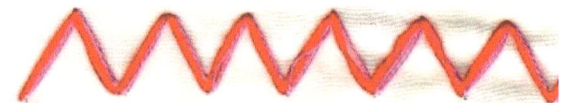

Arrowhead

Couched Arrowhead

Chain Stitch

Detached Chain Couching

1-2 Open Cretan

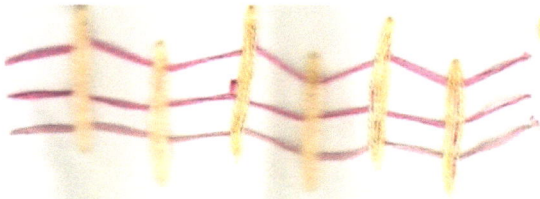

Open Cretan Overstitched

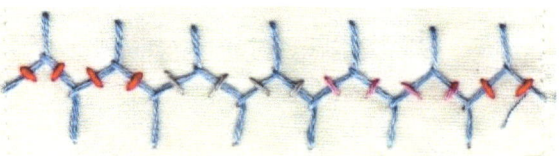

Couched Open Cretan

Couched Cross Stitch

Couched Cross Stitch

Cross Stitch

Couched Half Eyelet

Farmer's Day Crazy Quilt Stitches

Eyelet

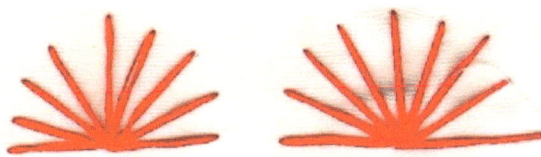

Half Eyelet

Couched Fan

Couched Straight Feather

Feather

Straight Feather

Open Fishbone

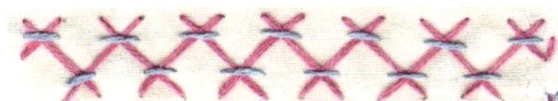

Couched Herringbone

Couched Herringbone

Herringbone

Sandwiched Herringbone

Shadow Herringbone

Couched Holbein

Ray

Ray

Buttonhole Scallop

Farmer's Day Crazy Quilt Stitches

Couched Straight Stitch

Straight Stitch

Straight Stitch

Combinations

Arrowhead and
Couched Line

Couched Arrowhead
and Small Arrowhead

Backstitch Rose

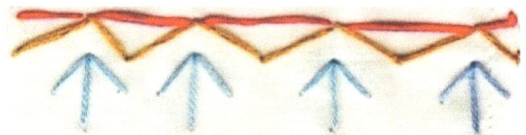

Backstitch, Arrowhead
and Arrow

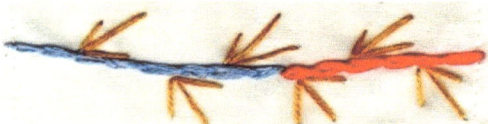

Chain and Arrow

Couched Cross Stitch
and Straight Stitch

Cross and
Straight Stitch

Couched Double Cross
and Arrow

Farmer's Day Crazy Quilt Stitches

Double Fan and Arrow

½ Pulled Straight Feather

Arrowhead, Stem Stitch and Straight Feather

Couched Elongated Double Feather

Pulled Straight Feather

Couched Open Fishbone and Arrowhead

Couched Herringbone, Arrow and Straight Stitch

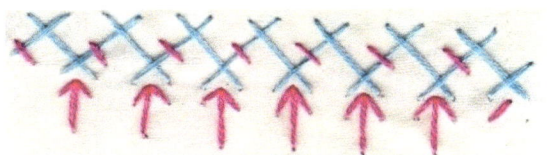

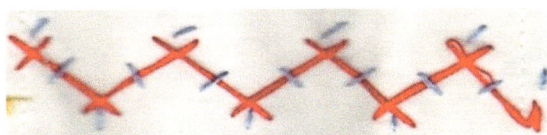

Couched Herringbone and Arrow

Couched Herringbone and Straight Stitch

Couched Herringbone and Straight Stitch

Couched Herringbone and Straight Stitch

Couched Herringbone and Straight Stitch

Farmer's Day Crazy Quilt Stitches

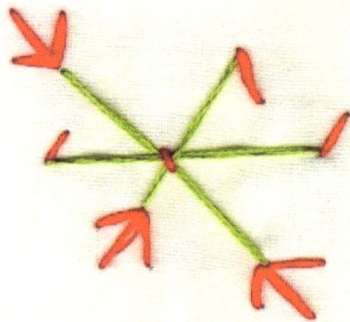

Couched Star and
Arrow

Backstitch and Lazy Daisy

Couching with Lazy Daisy
Fan and Herringbone

Trailing, Stem and
Straight Stitches

Shadow Herringbone and Arrow

Shadow Herringbone
and Straight Stitch

Couching with Herringbone,
Lazy Daisy Fan and Arrow

Lazy Daisy and French Knot

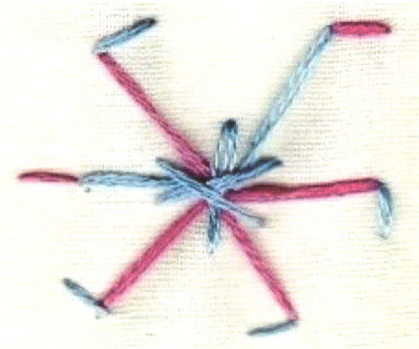

Double Wheel and
Straight Stitch

Military Ribbon Crazy Quilt

The distinguishing item of this quilt is an appliqued military ribbon with the printing "***Grand Army of the Republic, Grand Encampment***." The varied embroidery stitches are worked along seam lines only. The quilt contains cotton and silk fabrics. The backing is one piece of wool. There are no borders or batting. The binding is brought from the back to the front and hand stitched. The quilting is done by hand with dark brown thread and seven stitches to the inch.

The blocks are about 12" square with a straight set. The quilt is sewn by hand with a finished size of 47½" (length) by 37½" (width). It does not have a signature or date. This treasure is in poor condition.

Military Ribbon Crazy Quilt Stitches

Crossed Blanket

Detached Chain

Open Cretan

Mirrored Eyelet

Broken Feather

Simple Feather

Double Simple Feather

Straight Feather

Triple Feather

Spaced Triple Simple Feather

Mirrored Pulled Straight Feather

Double Herringbone

Combinations

½ Pulled Straight Feather and Lazy Daisy

½ Pulled Straight Feather and Lazy Daisy

Closed Pulled Straight Feather

Double Simple Feather and Lazy Daisy

Military Ribbon Quilt Stitches

Double Simple
Feather and Loops

Loops and Straight
Feather

Simple Feather
and Lazy Daisy

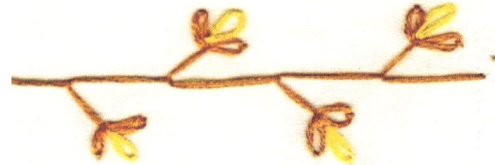

Spaced Simple Feather
and Lazy Daisy

Simple Feather and
Lazy Daisy Fan

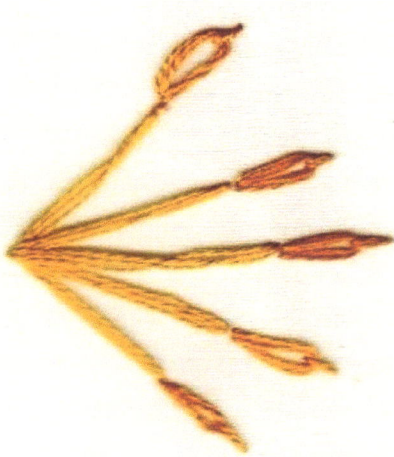

Fan and Lazy Daisy

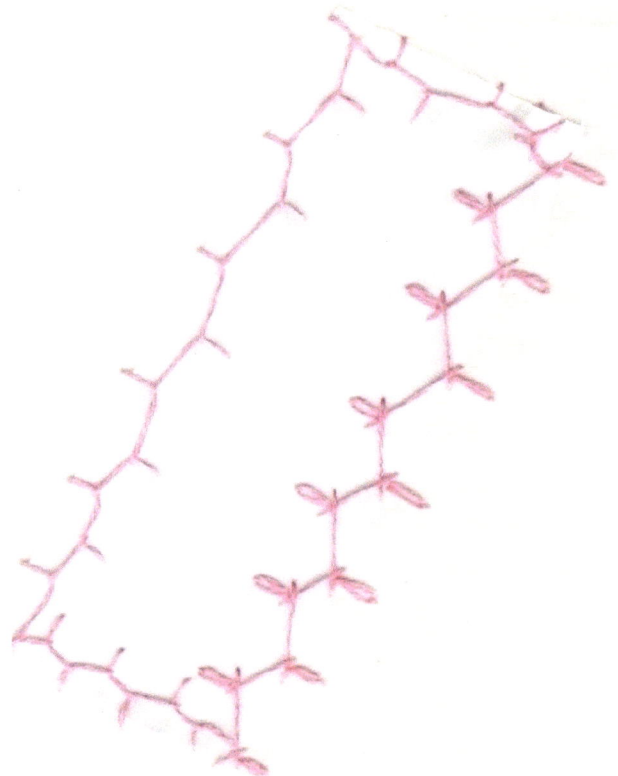

Open Cretan and Lazy Daisy

Herringbone and Lazy Daisy

Herringbone and Lazy Daisy

OWB Crazy Quilt

This wonderful crazy quilt features a variety of stitches worked along each seam line as well as making an eagle motif and fancy letters spelling "OWB". It also has four LeMoyne stars, a fan and an appliqued American flag. It is 63" x 49", has wool batting, was made circa 1900 and is in good condition.

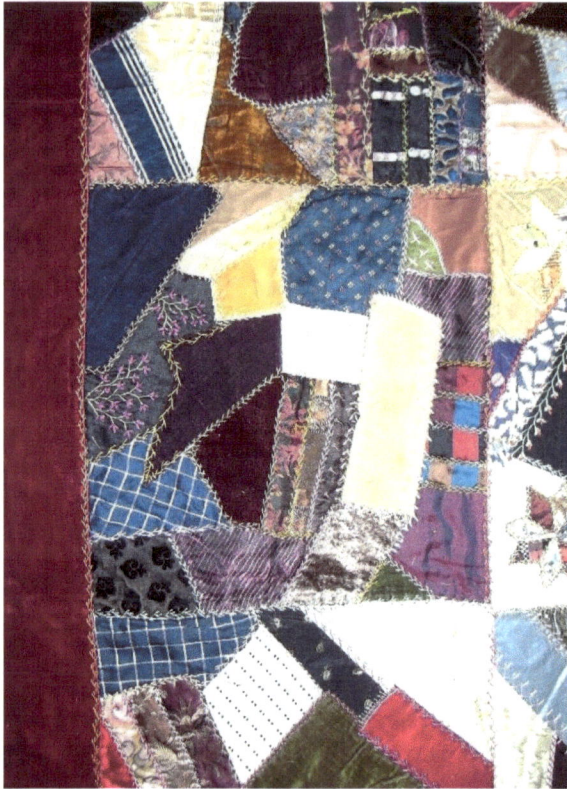

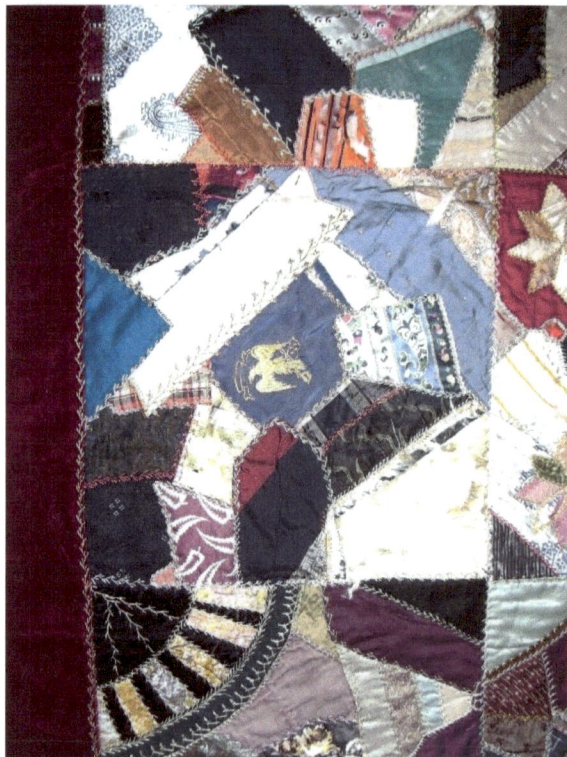

OWB Crazy Quilt Stitches

Arrow

Blanket

Leaning Blanket

Double Leaning Blanket

Long and Short Blanket

Varied Blanket Layered

Smyrna Cross

Feather

1-2 and Uneven
Elongated Feather

3-1 Simple Feather

Single Feather

Mirrored Single Feather

Mirrored Single
Feather Separated

Straight Feather

½ Pulled Straight Feather

½ Pulled Straight Feather

OWB Crazy Quilt Stitches

Double Straight Feather

Elongated Double Feather

Double Feather

Herringbone

Triple Feather

Combinations

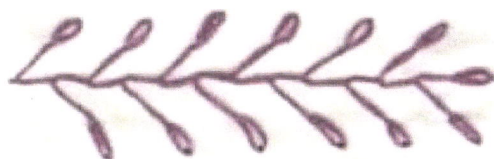

Simple Feather and
Lazy Daisy

Simple Feather and
Lazy Daisy

Chained Feather

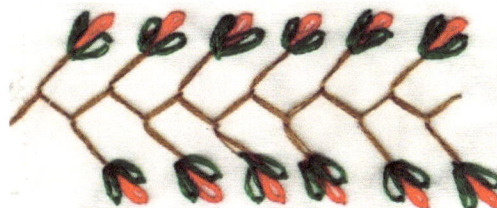

Feather and Lazy
Daisy Fan

Simple Feather
and Lazy Daisy

1-2 Simple Feather
and Lazy Daisy

OWB Crazy Quilt Stitches

Elongated Feather and Lazy Daisy Fan

3-1 Simple Feather
and Lazy Daisy

1-3 Simple Feather
and Lazy Daisy

Double Single Feather and
Lazy Daisy Fan

Herringbone and Lazy Daisy

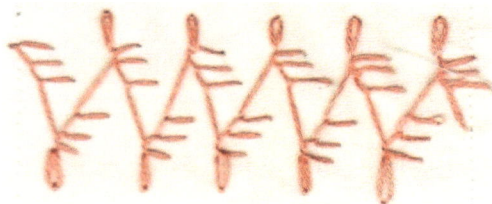

Triple Feather and Lazy
Daisy

Velvet Crazy Quilt

The Velvet Quilt is made of a glorious variety of velvet blocks, thus the name. The hand embroidery runs the gamut of stitch families in a riot of color and techniques. Motifs such as a blue bird, overlapping circles and concentric circles grace some of the patches. The size is approximately 68" x 56", there is no border, and it is tied. The quilt may have been made by a woman from Valparaiso circa 1961.

Velvet Crazy Quilt Stitches

Closed Blanket

Crossed Blanket

Stacked Blanket

Brick

Chain

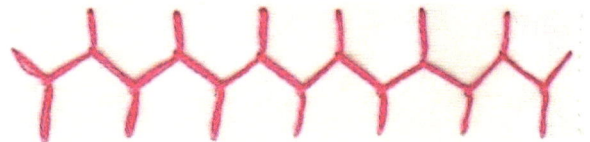

Open Cretan

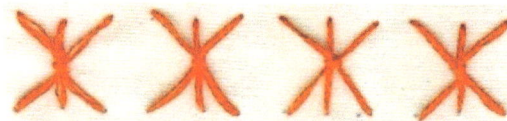

Three Leg Cross

Cross Stitch

Cross Stitch

Tacked Cross Stitch

Smyrna Cross

Pulled Straight Feather

Double Herringbone

Barbed Herringbone

Lazy Daisy Chain

Outline Stitch

Velvet Crazy Quilt Stitches

Sheaf

Stem

Combinations

Blanket Stitch Circle

Closed Blanket and Arrow

Closed Blanket and Lazy Daisy

Uneven Blanket Stitch and Upright Cross

Brick and Couched Cross

Barbed Chevron and French Knot

Cross Stitch and Lazy Daisy

Fan and French Knot

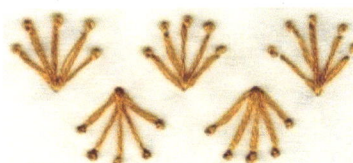

Fan and French Knot

Velvet Crazy Quilt Stitches

Fan and Straight Stitch

½ Pulled Layered Straight Feather

½ Pulled Straight Feather and ½ Feather

1/3 Pulled Triple Straight Feather and French Knot

Quad Feather and Smyrna Cross

Shadow Simple Feather and Lazy Daisy Fan

Lazy Daisy Fan, Straight Stitch and French Knot

Straight Stitch and Arrow

Outline, Straight, and Satin Stitches

Group	Sub Group	Stitch Name	LeMoyne Star	Farmer's Day	Military Ribbon	OWB	Velvet
Arrow		Arrow	LEM	FARM		OWB	
Arrow		Arrowhead		FARM			
Arrow		Couched Arrowhead		FARM			
Arrow		Stacked Arrowhead	LEM				
Arrow		Two Color Arrowhead	LEM	FARM			
Blanket		2 Color Layered Blanket	LEM				
Blanket		Blanket	LEM			OWB	
Blanket		Closed Blanket					VEL
Blanket		Crossed Blanket			MR		VEL
Blanket		Double Leaning Blanket				OWB	
Blanket		Leaning Blanket				OWB	
Blanket		Long and Short Blanket	LEM			OWB	
Blanket		Stacked Blanket					VEL
Blanket		Varied Blanket Layered				OWB	
Brick		Brick					VEL
Chain		Chain	LEM	FARM			VEL
Chain		Detached Chain			MR		
Chain		Detached Twisted Chain	LEM				
Chain		Detached Chain Couching		FARM			
Cretan		1-2 Open Cretan		FARM			
Cretan		Couched Open Cretan		FARM			
Cretan		Cretan Variation		FARM			
Cretan		Open Cretan			MR		VEL
Cretan		Open Cretan Overstitched		FARM			
Cretan		Overstacked Cretan		FARM			
Cretan		Mirrored Cretan	LEM				
Cretan		Tied Cretan		FARM			
Cross		Cross Stitch	LEM	FARM			VEL
Cross		Couched Cross		FARM			
Cross		Double Cross	LEM				
Cross		Smyrna Cross				OWB	VEL
Cross		Three Leg Cross					VEL
Cross		Tacked					VEL
Eyelet		Couched Half Eyelet		FARM			
Eyelet		Eyelet		FARM			
Eyelet		Eyelet and French Knots	LEM				
Eyelet		Half Eyelet		FARM			
Eyelet		Mirrored Eyelet			MR		
Fan		Couched Fan		FARM			
Feather		1-2 and Uneven Elongated Feather				OWB	
Feather		1-2 Extended Feather	LEM				
Feather		Broken Feather			MR		
Feather		Extended Feather Layered	LEM				
Feather		Feather		FARM			

Group	Sub Group	Stitch Name	LeMoyne Star	Farmer's Day	Military Ribbon	OWB	Velvet
Feather		Triple Feather	LEM		MR	OWB	
Feather - Simple		1-2 Simple Feather	LEM				
Feather - Simple		1-3 Simple Feather	LEM				
Feather - Simple		3-1 Simple Feather				OWB	
Feather - Simple		Double Simple Feather	LEM		MR		
Feather - Simple		Simple Feather	LEM		MR		
Feather - Simple		Spaced Triple Simple Feather			MR		
Feather - Simple		Triple Simple Feather	LEM				
Feather - Simple		Uneven Triple Simple Feather	LEM				
Feather - Single		Alternating Single Feather				OWB	
Feather - Single		Mirrored Single Feather	LEM			OWB	
Feather - Single		Single Feather	LEM			OWB	
Feather - Straight		1/2 Pulled Straight Feather				OWB	
Feather - Straight		Closed Straight Feather	LEM				
Feather - Straight		Couched Straight Feather		FARM			
Feather - Straight		Double Straight Feather	LEM			OWB	
Feather - Straight		Pulled Straight Feather					VEL
Feather - Straight		Straight Feather	LEM	FARM	MR	OWB	
Feather - Double		Double Feather	LEM			OWB	
Feather - Double		Elongated Double Feather				OWB	
Feather - Double		Mirrored Double Feather	LEM				
Fishbone		Open Fishbone		FARM			
Fly		Fly	LEM				
Fly		Boxed Fly	LEM				
Fly		Stacked Fly	LEM				
Fly		Stacked Fly Variations	LEM				
French Knot		French Knot	LEM	FARM	MR	OWB	VEL
Herringbone		Barbed Herringbone					VEL
Herringbone		Couched Herringbone		FARM			
Herringbone		Double Herringbone			MR		VEL
Herringbone		Herringbone		FARM		OWB	
Herringbone		Mirrored Herringbone and French Knot	LEM				
Herringbone		Sandwiched Herringbone		FARM			

Group	Sub Group	Stitch Name	LeMoyne Star	Farmer's Day	Military Ribbon	OWB	Velvet
Herringbone		Shadow Herringbone	LEM	FARM			
Holbein		Couched Holbein		FARM			
Holbein		Stacked Holbein Stitch	LEM				
Lazy Daisy		Lazy Daisy Chain					VEL
Lazy Daisy		Lazy Daisy Flower Chain	LEM				
Outline		Outline Stitch					VEL
Ray		Ray		FARM			
Satin Stitch		Satin Stitch		FARM			
Sheaf		Sheaf					VEL
Stem		Stem					VEL
Straight Stitch		Couched Straight Stitch		FARM			
Straight Stitch		Straight Stitch		FARM			
Straight Stitch		Straight Stitch Knot	LEM				
Y		Y Stitch	LEM				

Combination Stitches

Group	Sub Group	Stitch Name	LeMoyne Star	Farmer's Day	Military Ribbon	OWB	Velvet
Combination	Arrowhead	Arrowhead and Arrow	LEM				
Combination	Arrowhead	Arrowhead and Couched Line		FARM			
Combination	Arrowhead	Couched Arrowhead and Small Arrowhead		FARM			
Combination	Arrowhead	Stacked Arrow and Arrowhead	LEM				
Combination	Arrowhead	Y Stitch and Arrowhead	LEM				
Combination	Arrowhead	Y Stitch and Two Color Arrowhead	LEM				
Combination	Backstitch	Backstitch Rose		FARM			
Combination	Backstitch	Backstitch, Arrowhead and Arrow		FARM			
Combination	Blanket	Blanket and Straight Stitch	LEM				
Combination	Blanket	Blanket Stitch Circle					VEL
Combination	Blanket	Closed Blanket and Arrow					VEL
Combination	Blanket	Closed Blanket and Lazy Daisy					VEL
Combination	Blanket	Sheaf, Blanket and French Knot	LEM				
Combination	Blanket	Uneven Blanket Stitch and Upright Cross					VEL
Combination	Brick	Brick and Couched Cross					VEL
Combination	Chain	Chain and Arrow		FARM			
Combination	Chevron	Barbed Chevron and French Knot					VEL
Combination	Cretan	Mirrored Open Cretan	LEM				
Combination	Cretan	Open Cretan and Arrow	LEM				
Combination	Cross	Couched Cross Stitch and Straight Stitch		FARM			
Combination	Cross	Cross Stitch and Lazy Daisy					VEL
Combination	Cross	Cross and Straight Stitch		FARM			
Combination	Cross	Cross Stitch and Arrow	LEM				
Combination	Cross	Cross Stitch and Straight Stitch	LEM				
Combination	Cross	Cross Stitch Line and French Knot	LEM				

Group	Sub Group	Stitch Name	LeMoyne Star	Farmer's Day	Military Ribbon	OWB	Velvet
Combination	Cross	Y Stitch and Cross	LEM				
Combination	Double Cross	Couched Double Cross and Arrow		FARM			
Combination	Fan	Double Fan and Arrow		FARM			
Combination	Fan	Fan and French Knot					VEL
Combination	Fan	Fan and Straight Stitch					VEL
Combination	Feather	1/2 Pulled Layered Straight Feather					VEL
Combination	Feather	1/2 Pulled Straight Feather		FARM			
Combination	Feather	1/2 pulled Straight Feather and 1/2 Feather					VEL
Combination	Feather	1/2 pulled Straight Feather and Lazy Daisy			MR		
Combination	Feather	1/3 Pulled Triple Straight Feather and French Knot					VEL
Combination	Feather	2-3 Simple Feather and Lazy Daisy	LEM				
Combination	Feather	Angled Double Single Feather, Straight Stitch, and Couching	LEM				
Combination	Feather	Arrowhead, Stem Stitch and Straight Feather		FARM			
Combination	Feather	Chained Feather				OWB	
Combination	Feather	Closed Pulled Straight Feather			MR		
Combination	Feather	Couched Elongated Double Feather		FARM			
Combination	Feather	Cross Stitch and Feather	LEM				
Combination	Feather	Double Simple Feather and Lazy Daisy			MR		
Combination	Feather	Double Simple Feather and Loops			MR		
Combination	Feather	Elongated Feather and Lazy Daisy Fan				OWB	
Combination	Feather	Feather and French Knot	LEM				
Combination	Feather	Feather and Lazy Daisy Fan	LEM			OWB	
Combination	Feather	Feather Circles and French Knots	LEM				
Combination	Feather	Feather, Loop and Uneven Fan	LEM				
Combination	Feather	Loops and Straight Feather			MR		
Combination	Feather	Mirrored Pulled Straight Feather			MR		
Combination	Feather	Piled Simple Feather and Lazy Daisy Fan	LEM				
Combination	Feather	Pulled Straight Feather		FARM			
Combination	Feather	Quad Feather and Smyrna Cross					VEL
Combination	Feather	Shadow Simple Feather and Lazy Daisy Fan					VEL
Combination	Feather	Simple Feather and Lazy Daisy	LEM		MR	OWB	
Combination	Feather	Simple Feather and Lazy Daisy Fan			MR		
Combination	Feather	Simple Feather and Lazy Daisy Fans	LEM		MR		
Combination	Feather	Single Feather and Lazy Daisy	LEM				
Combination	Feather	Spaced Simple Feather and Lazy Daisy			MR		
Combination	Feather	Straight Feather, Lazy Daisy and French Knot	LEM				
Combination	Feather	Triple Feather and Lazy Daisy	LEM				
Combination	Feather	Uneven Triple Feather and Lazy Daisy	LEM				
Combination	Feather - Simple	1-2 Simple Feather and Lazy Daisy				OWB	
Combination	Feather - Simple	1-3 Simple Feather and Lazy Daisy				OWB	
Combination	Feather - Simple	3-1 Simple Feather and Lazy Daisy				OWB	

Group	Sub Group	Stitch Name	LeMoyne Star	Farmer's Day	Military Ribbon	OWB	Velvet
Combination	Feather - Single	Double Single Feather and Lazy Daisy Fan				OWB	
Combination	Feather - Triple	Triple Feather and Lazy Daisy				OWB	
Combination	Fishbone	Couched Open Fishbone and Arrowhead		FARM			
Combination	Fly	Fly and Slipped Straight Stitch	LEM				
Combination	Herringbone	Couched Herringbone and Arrow		FARM			
Combination	Herringbone	Couched Herringbone and Straight Stitch		FARM			
Combination	Herringbone	Couched Herringbone, Arrow and Straight Stitch		FARM			
Combination	Herringbone	Double Herringbone and French Knot		FARM			
Combination	Herringbone	Herringbone and Lazy Daisy	LEM	FARM	MR	OWB	
Combination	Herringbone	Shadow Herringbone and Arrow		FARM			
Combination	Herringbone	Shadow Herringbone and Straight Stitch		FARM			
Combination	Lazy Daisy	Lazy Daisy Fan, Straight Stitch and French Knot					VEL
Combination	Lazy Daisy	Backstitch and Lazy Daisy		FARM			
Combination	Lazy Daisy	Couched with Lazy Daisy Fan and Herringbone		FARM			
Combination	Lazy Daisy	Couching with Herringbone, Lazy Daisy Fan and Arrow		FARM			
Combination	Lazy Daisy	Open Cretan and Lazy Daisy			MR		
Combination	Lazy Daisy	Fan and Lazy Daisy			MR		
Combination	Lazy Daisy	Lazy Daisy and French Knot	LEM	FARM			
Combination	Nun's Stitch	Nun's Stitch and Lazy Daisy	LEM				
Combination	Outline	Outline, Straight, and Satin Stitches					VEL
Combination	Star	Couched Star and Arrow		FARM			
Combination	Straight	Straight Stitch and Arrow					VEL
Combination	Trailing	Trailing, Stem, and Straight Stitches		FARM			
Combination	Wheel	Double Wheel and Straight Stitch		FARM			

Instructions for Embroidery Stitches

Introduction

In keeping with the hand sewing of antique crazy quilts, the directions are hand embroidered and hand drawn by the author. Each stitch begins with a hand embroidered sample. This is followed by a "stitch map" that shows the path that the needle will take. That journey then goes step by step to show where the needle and thread are placed to begin and end the stitch. Numbers direct the sequences with the needle coming up through the fabric from the back at each odd number and going down through the fabric at the even numbers. Sometimes the needle goes through the same hole two or more times. This spot can be indicated by either an * or a series of numbers such as 1 /2 or 2 / 4 / 6. The working thread may be over or under the needle's point or wrapped around it. It can also be held above or below the stitching line.

EXAMPLE: Simple Feather Stitch

Embroidered
Sample

Tip

All odd numbers have the needle coming up through the underside of the cloth.

All even numbers have the needle going down through the top of the cloth.

Stitch Map

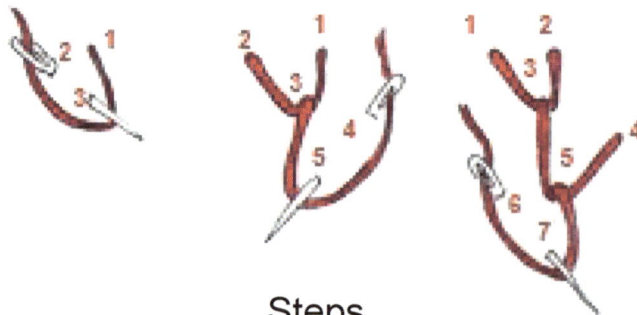

Steps

Blanket Stitches

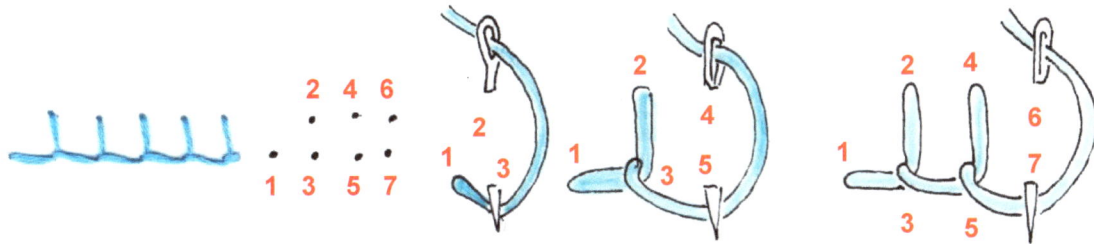

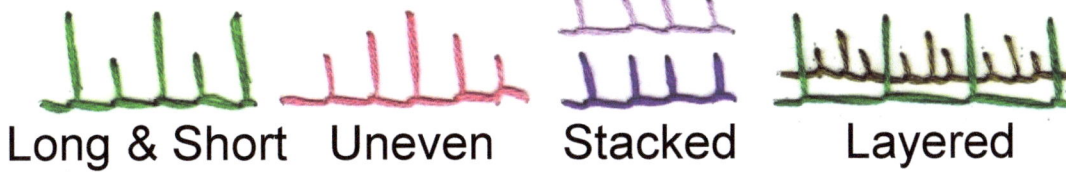

Long & Short   Uneven   Stacked   Layered

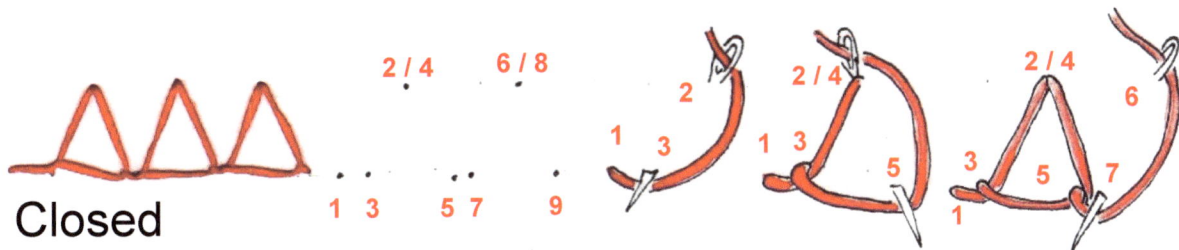

Closed

Crossed

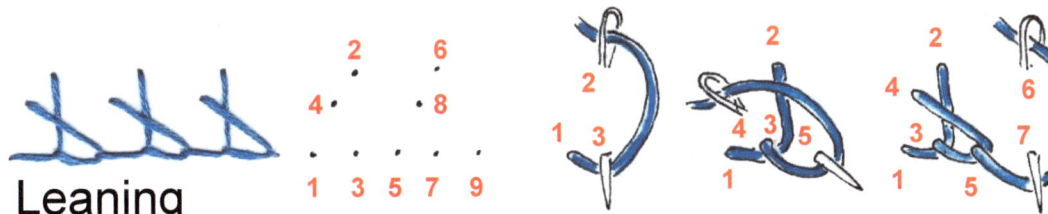

Leaning

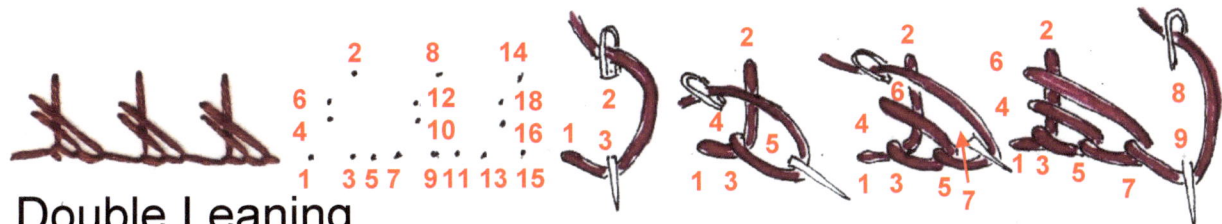

Double Leaning

Chain Stitches

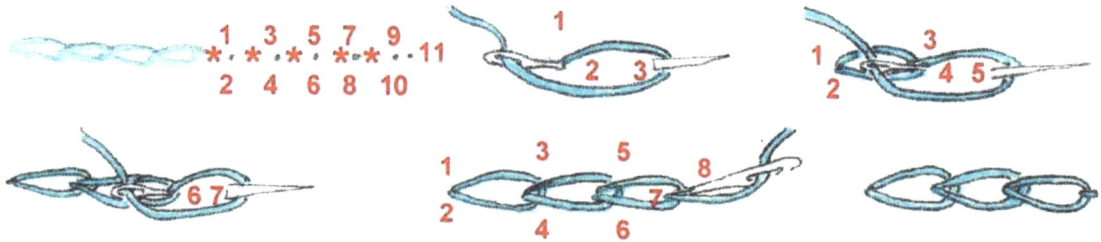

* The needle goes into each hole twice

Basic

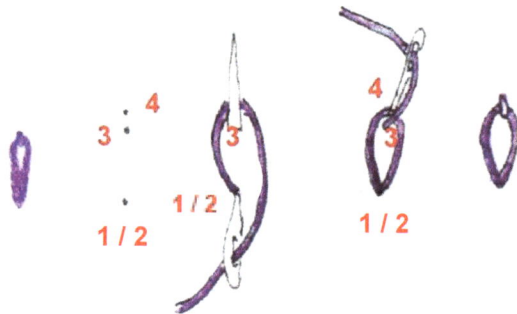

Lazy Daisy

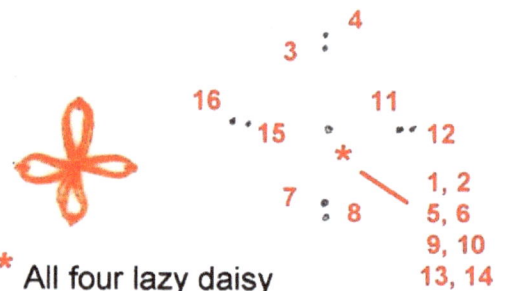

* All four lazy daisy stitches start in the center hole.

Lazy Daisy Flower

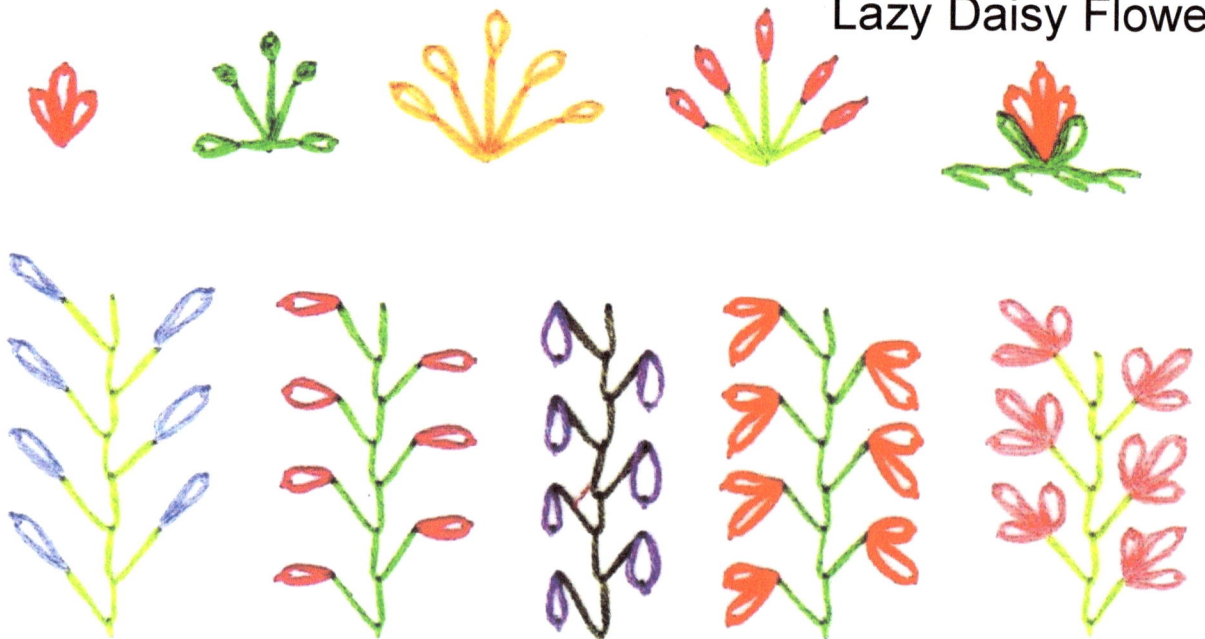

Couching

Basic couching is a two step technique in which a thread is brought up at the beginning of the design and laid along the design line. A second thread and needle are used to sew evenly spaced small straight stitches across the laid thread to fasten it down to the background fabric. The couching thread may be the same or different color as the laid thread. The laid thread comes through the fabric only at the beginning and end of the design line. Variations include puffing or looping the laid thread and using other embroidery stitches to tie one or more laid threads down. A and B indicate the laid thread.

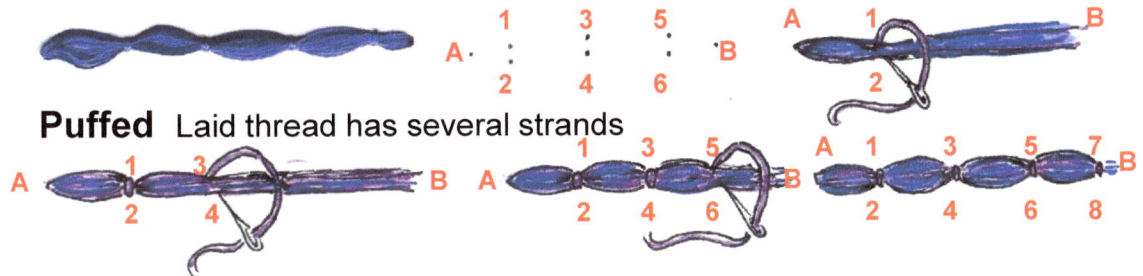

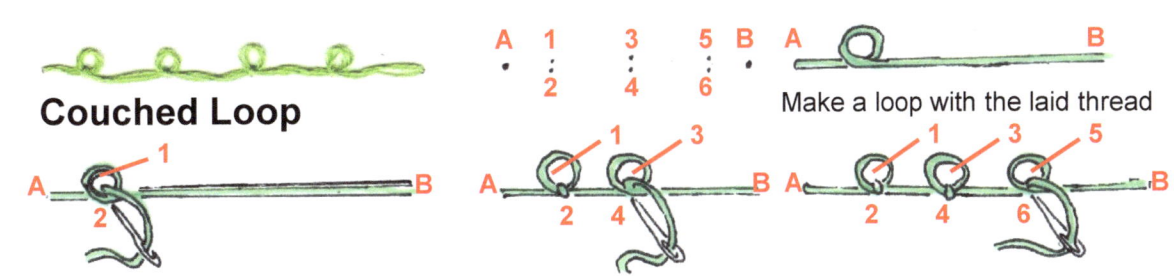

Basic

Puffed Laid thread has several strands

Couched Loop

Make a loop with the laid thread

Open Cretan Stitches

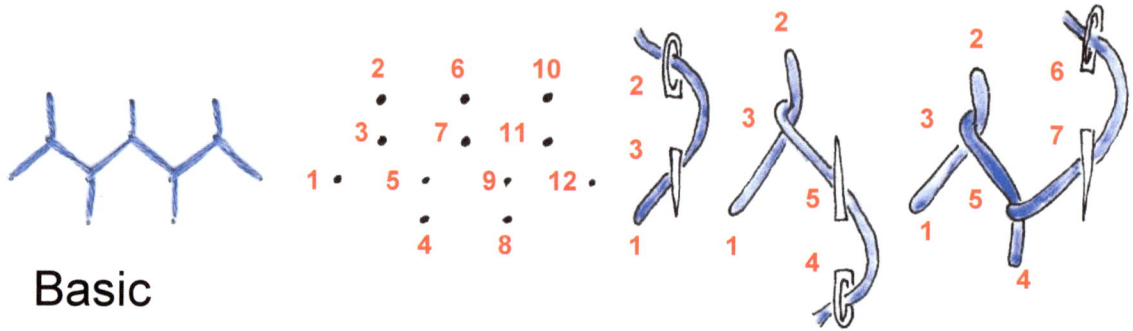

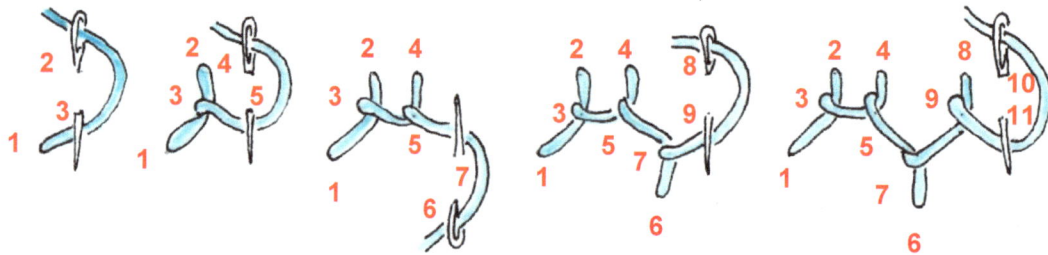

Basic

2-1 Variation

Variations with arrows, different sizes and locations

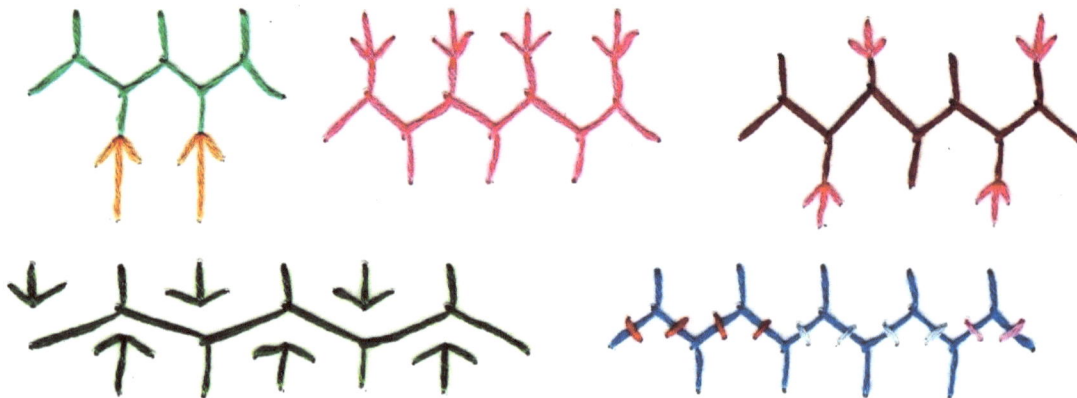

Expanded   Tied

Open Cretan Stitches

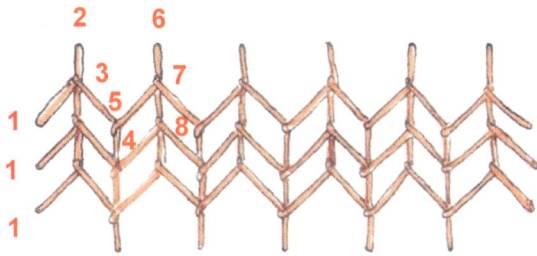

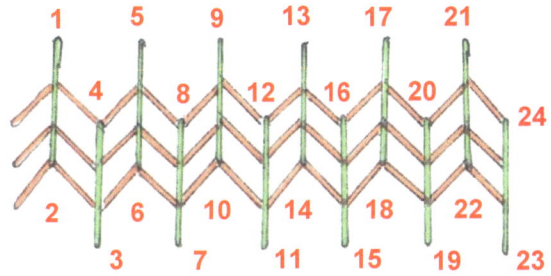

Stacked 3 Rows

Follow the same pattern, starting at 1, for each row

Overstitched Stacked

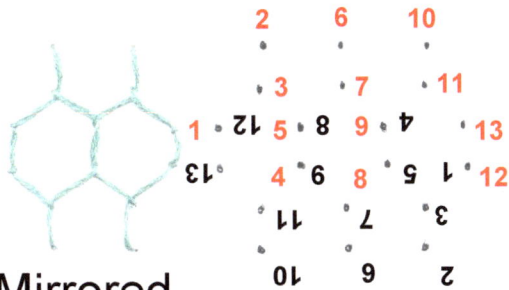

Mirrored

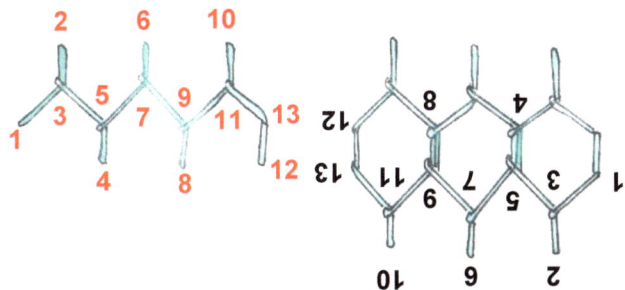

Turn fabric upside down to make the second series. Black numbers are upside down to represent the second series. The two middle rows in the stitch map have shared holes (red and black numbers) except for hole 13, which is single.

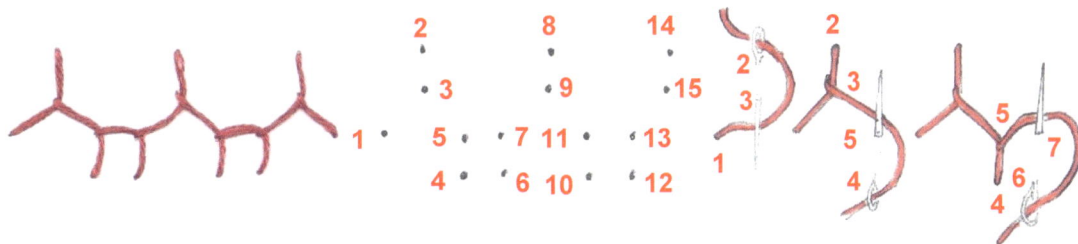

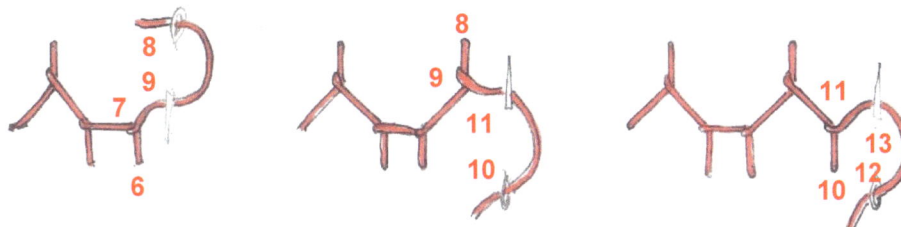

1 – 2 Variation

Cross Stitches

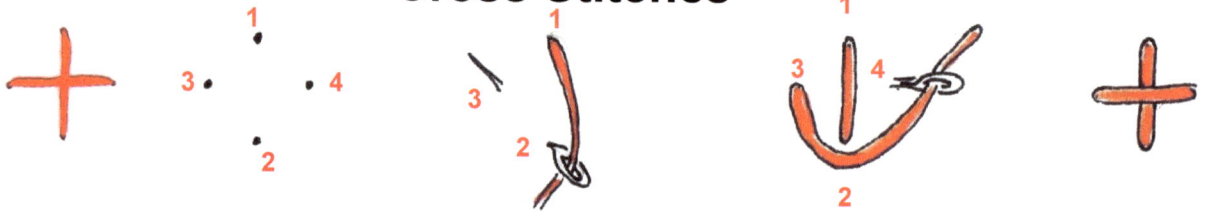

Upright Cross

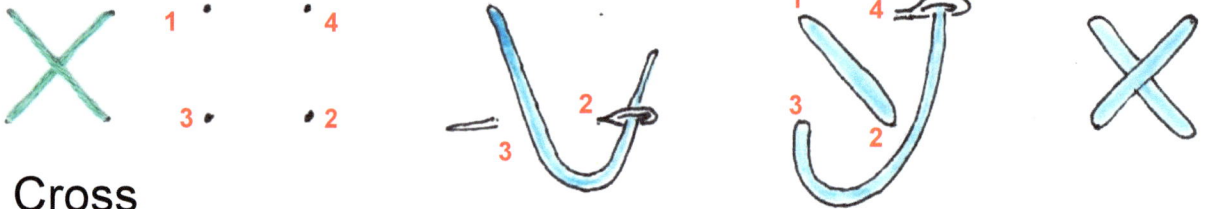

Cross

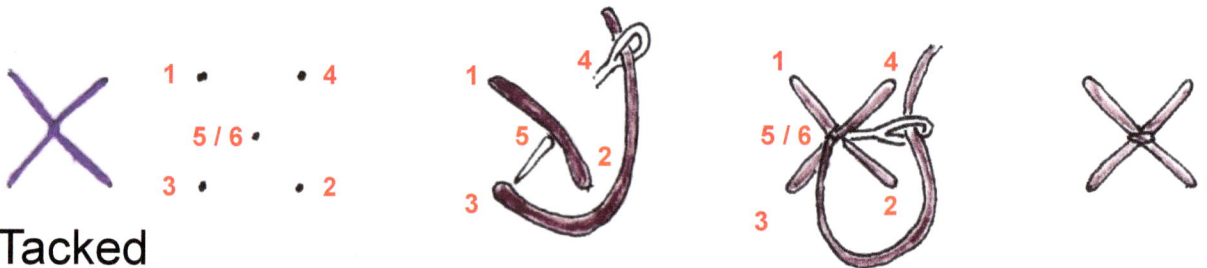

Tacked

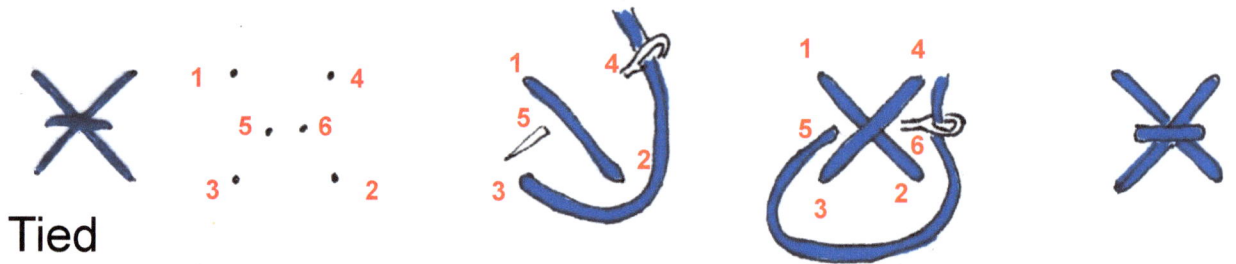

Tied

Smyrna Cross X +

Double Cross + X

Feather Stitches

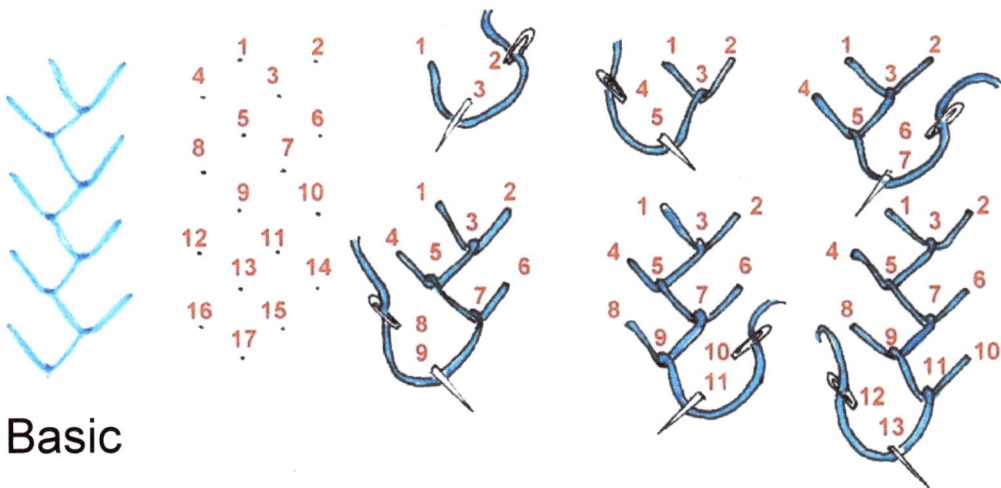

Basic

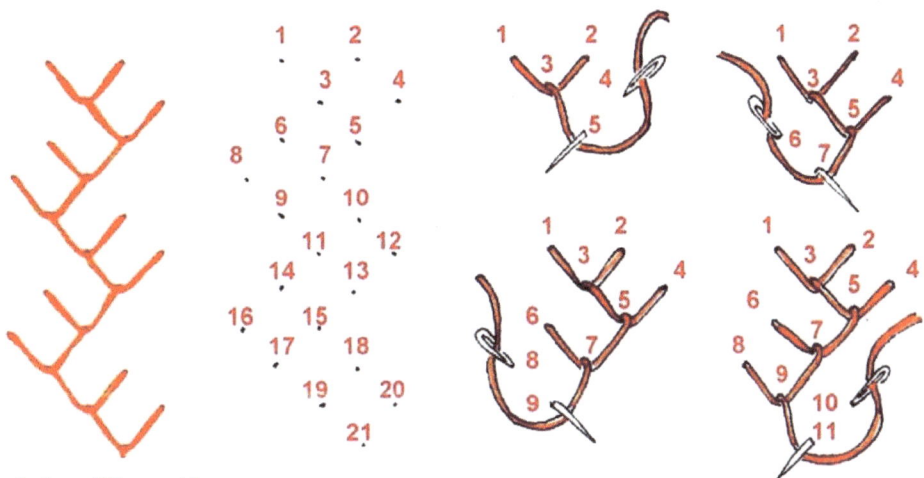

Double Feather

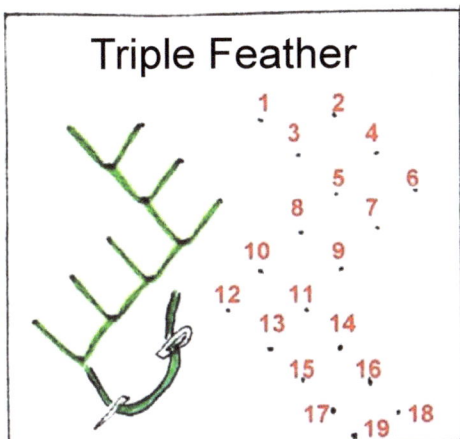

Triple Feather

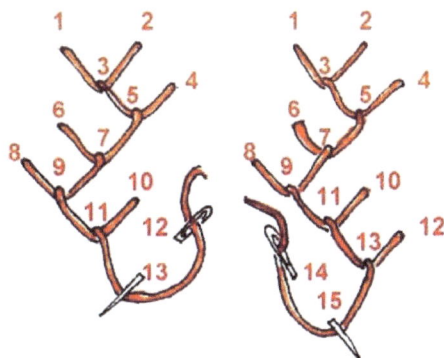

Simple Feather Stitches

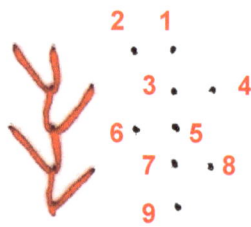  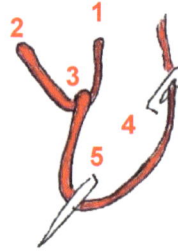 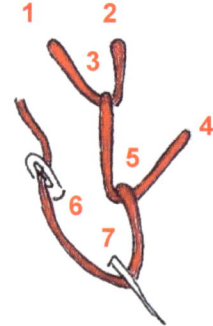

Basic

Variations

 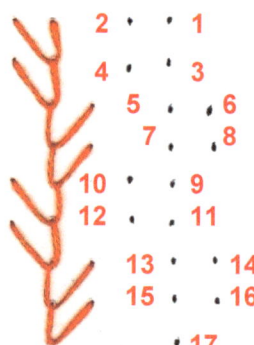 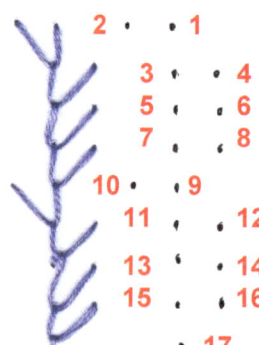 

1-2   Double   1-3   2-3

Elongated   With lazy daisy added

Single Feather Stitches (or Slanted Blanket)

Mirrored

2 •	• 1	
4 •	• 3	
6 •	• 5	
8 •	• 7	
10 •	• 9	
12 •	• 11	
	• 13	

1 •	• 2	
3 •	• 4	
5 •	• 6	
7 •	• 8	
9 •	• 10	
11 •		

Alternating

2 •	• 1
4 •	• 3
6 •	• 5
8 •	• 7
9 •	• 10
11 •	• 12
13 •	• 14
15 •	• 16
18 •	• 17
20 •	• 19
22 •	• 21
24 •	• 23
	• 25

1 •	• 2
3 •	• 4
5 •	• 6
7 •	• 8
10 •	• 9
12 •	• 11
14 •	• 13
16 •	• 15
17 •	• 18
19 •	• 20
21 •	• 22
23 •	• 24
25 •	

Straight Feather Stitches

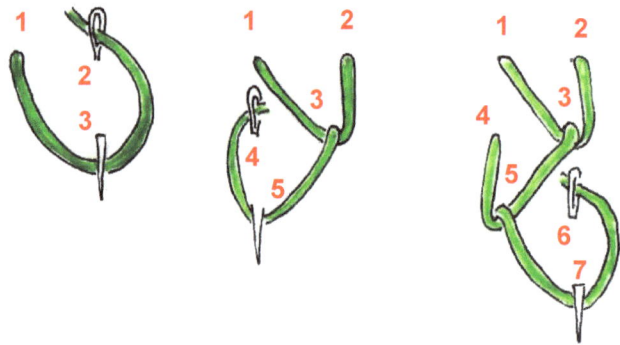

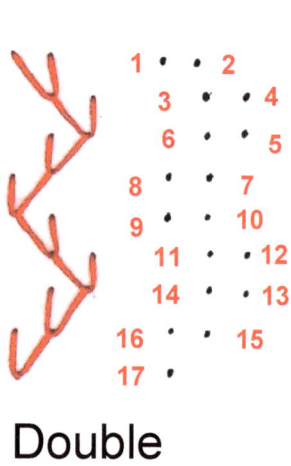

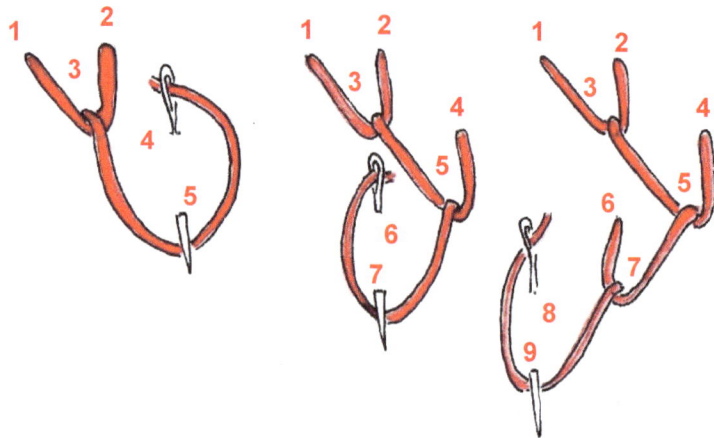

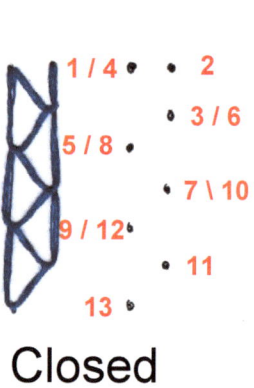

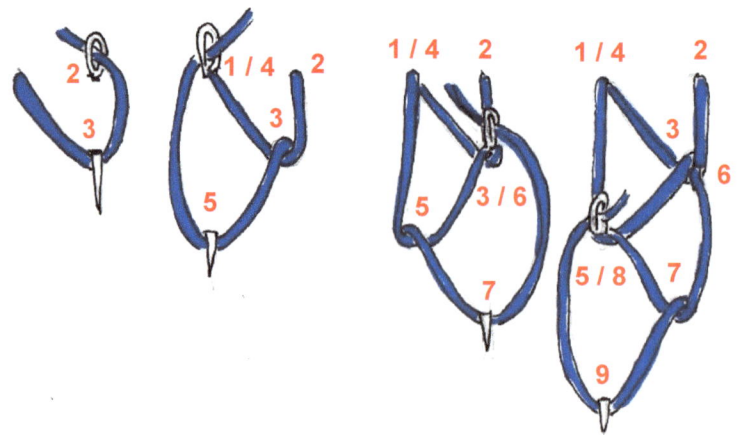

Basic

Double

Closed

Pulled Straight Feather Stitches

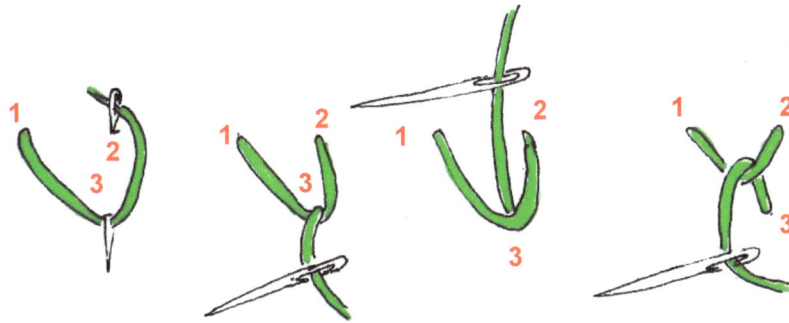

Basic

Pull working thread up away from 3 to reduce amount of thread from 1 to 2.

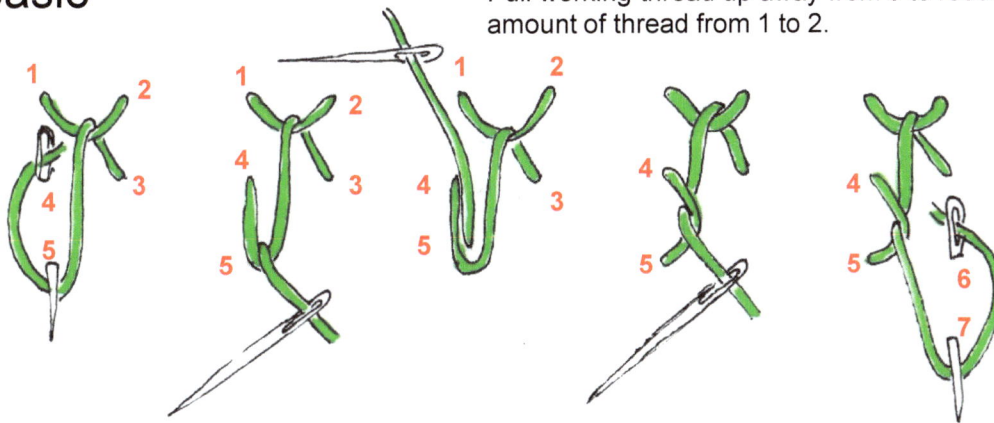

Pull working thread up away from 5 to reduce amount of thread from 4 to 5.

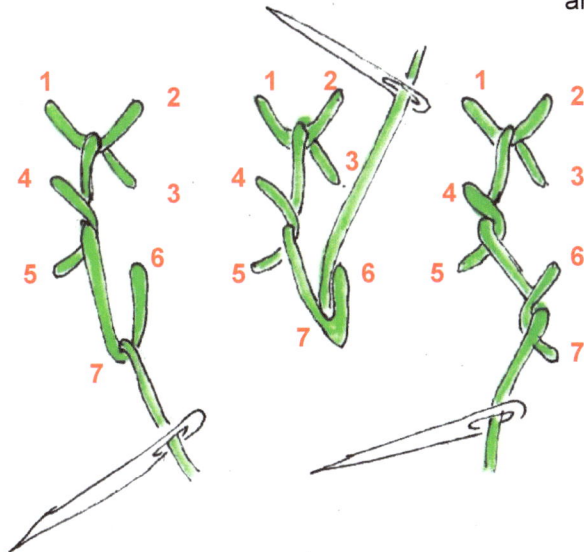

Pull working thread up to reduce amount of thread from 6 to 7.

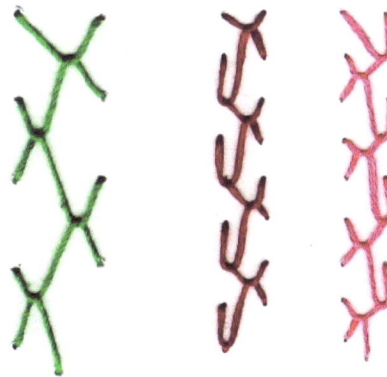

Basic	½ Pulled Right	½ Pulled Left

Fly Stitches

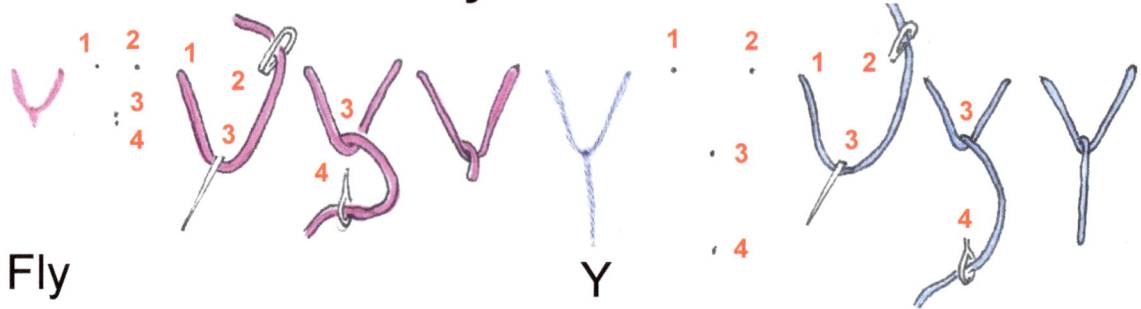

Fly   Y

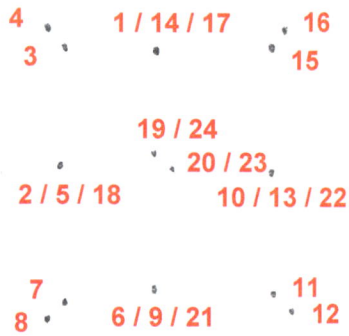

An extended fly has a wider angle like a corner of a square. The boxed has a fly at each corner and mirrored fly stitches in the center. Most holes are used more than once.

Stacked Fly

Stacked Fly Variation

Boxed Fly

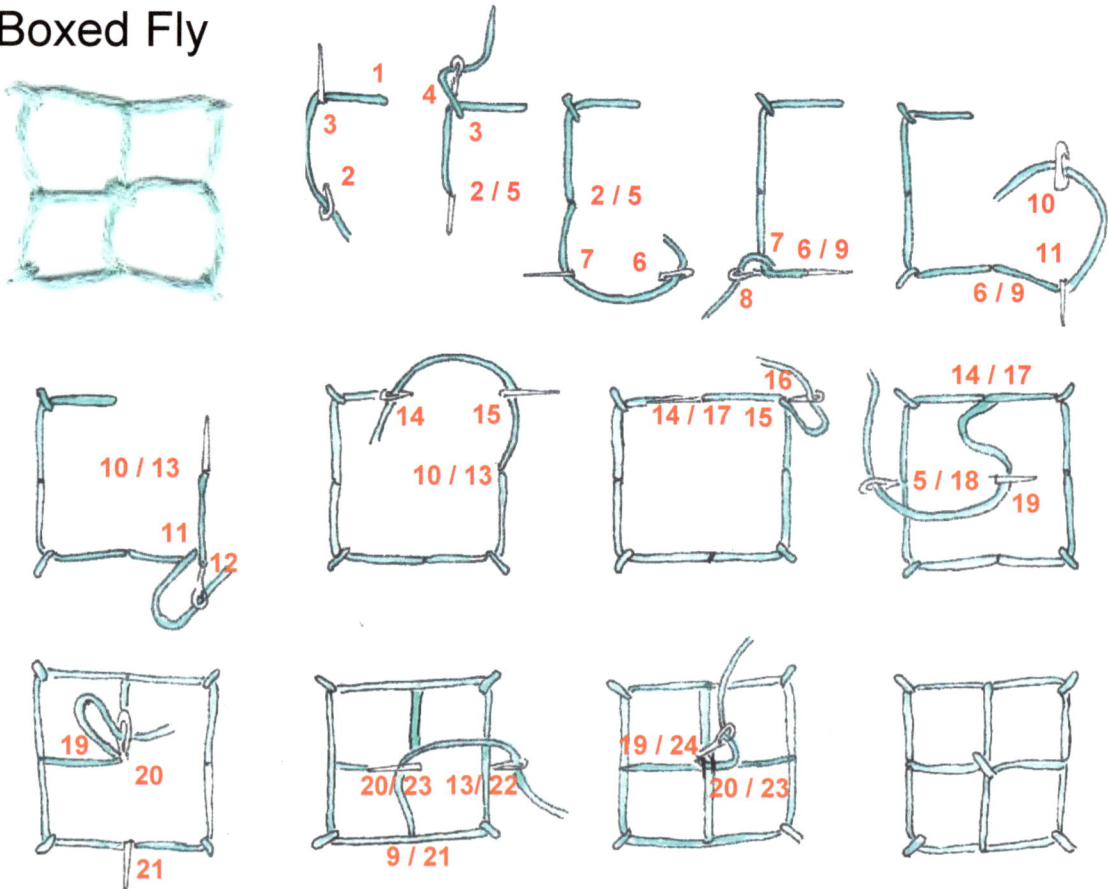

Herringbone Stitches

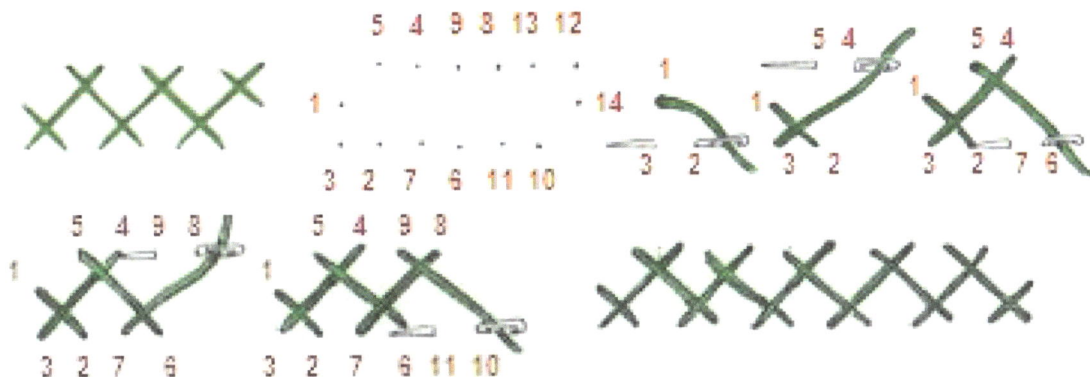

5　4　9　3　13　12

1

14

1

3　2　7　6　11　10

5　4

5　4

1

3　2

3　2

3　2　7　6

5　4　9　3

5　4　9　3

1

1

3　2　7　6

3　2　7　6　11　10

Basic with Compensating Stitches

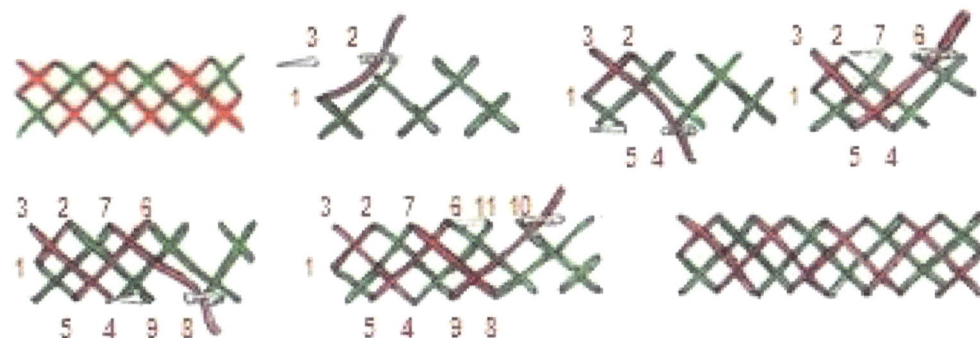

3　2

3　2

3　2　7　6

1

1

5　4

5　4

3　2　7　6

3　2　7　6　11　10

1

1

5　4　9　3

5　4　9　3

2 Color Closed Herringbone

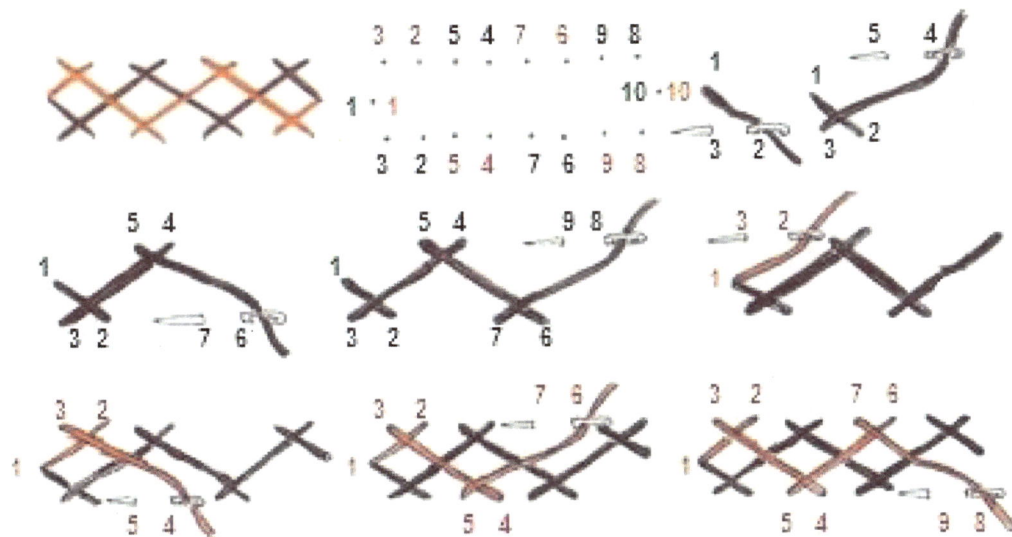

3　2　5　4　7　6　9　8

1

10　10

5　4

1　1

1

3　2　5　4　7　6　9　8

3　2

3

5　4

5　4

9　8

3　2

1

1

1

3　2

7　6

3　2

7　6

3　2

7　6

3　2

7　6

1

1

5　4

5　4

5　4

9　8

2 Color Elongated Herringbone

3 journeys, 3 colors
Shadow

3 journeys, 2 colors　　3 journeys, 3 colors
Sandwiched

Holbein Stitch (or Double Running)

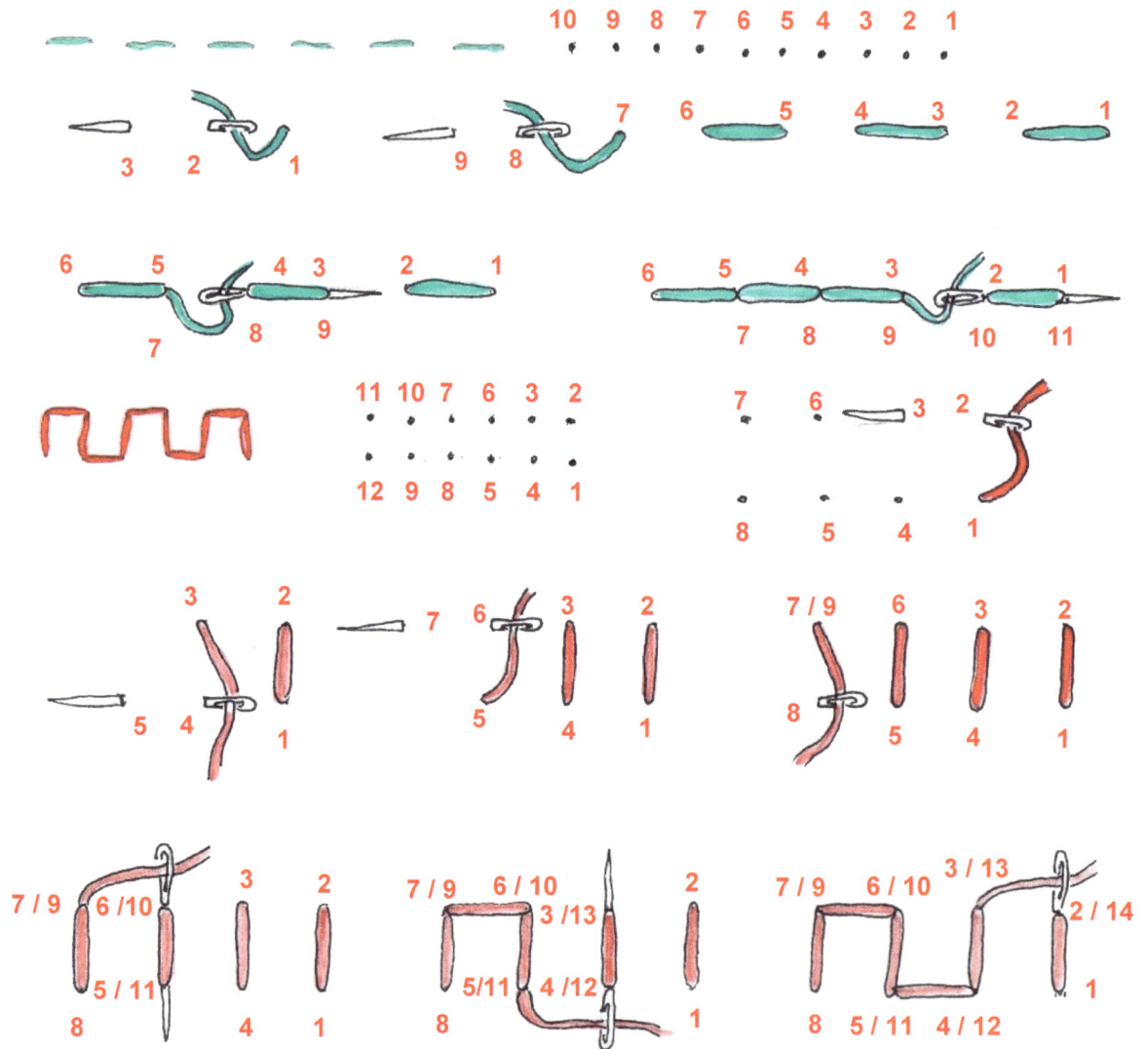

10 9 8 7 6 5 4 3 2 1

3 2 1   9 8 7   6   5   4   3   2   1

6   5   4 3   2   1   6   5   4   3   2   1
7   8 9   7   8   9   10   11

11 10 7 6 3 2   7   6   3   2

12 9 8 5 4 1   8   5   4   1

3   2   7 6   3   2   7 / 9   6   3   2

5 4   1   5   4   1   8   5   4   1

7 / 9   6 /10   3   2   7 / 9   6 / 10   3 /13   2   7 / 9   6 / 10   3 / 13   2 / 14

5 / 11   5/11   4 /12   8   5 / 11   4 / 12   1

8   4   1   8   1

Second journey left to right shares holes as shown 7/9 and 6/10.

Single   2 Colors Stacked   3 Colors Stacked

Line Stitches

Outline Stitch

Working thread is always above the needle. Stitch line starts on the fabric left side and progresses going right.

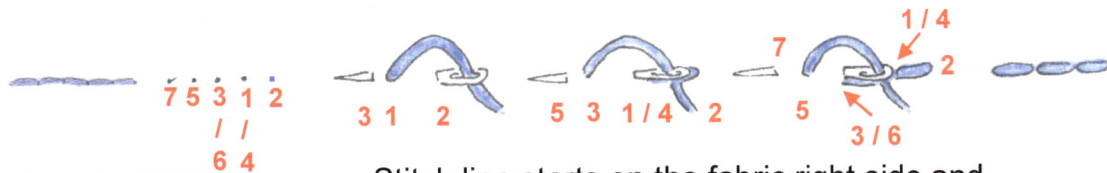

Stem Stitch

Working thread is always below the needle. Stitch line starts on the fabric left side and progresses going right.

Back Stitch

Stitch line starts on the fabric right side and progresses going left.

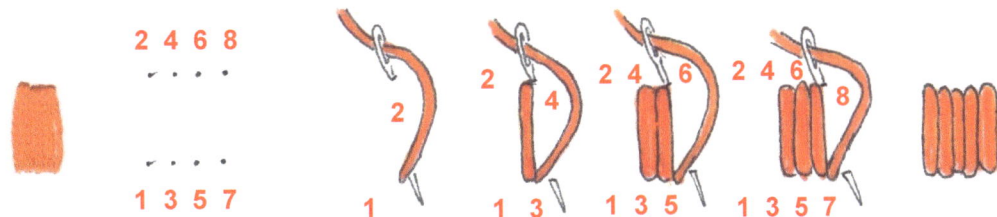

Running Stitch

Stitch line starts on the fabric right side and progresses going left.

Satin Stitch

Miscellaneous Stitches

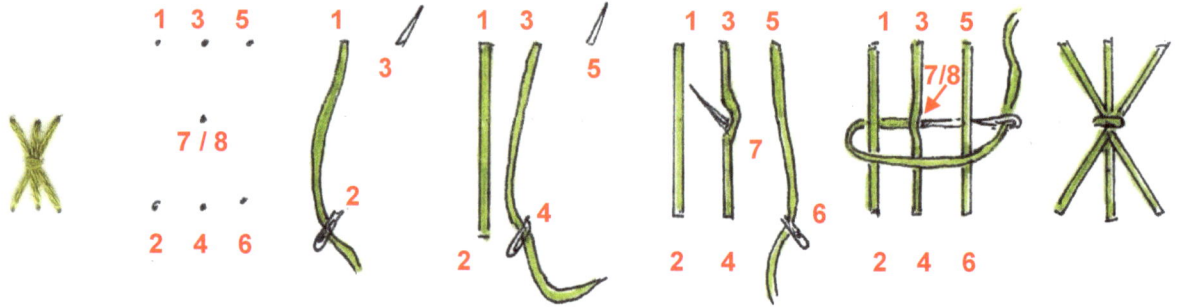

Sheaf Stitch

Eyelet Stitch

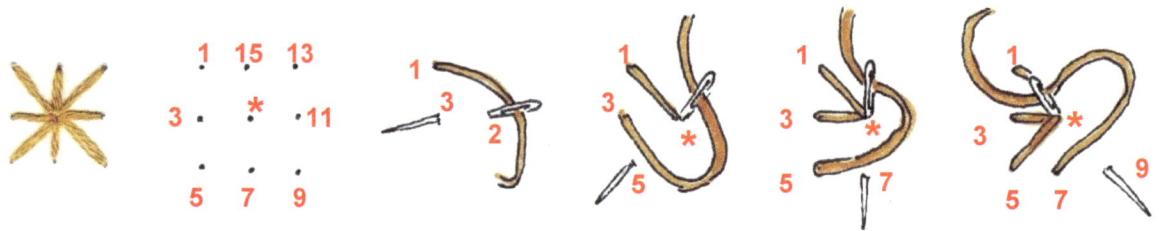

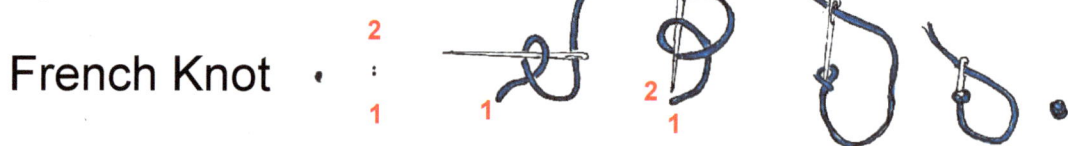

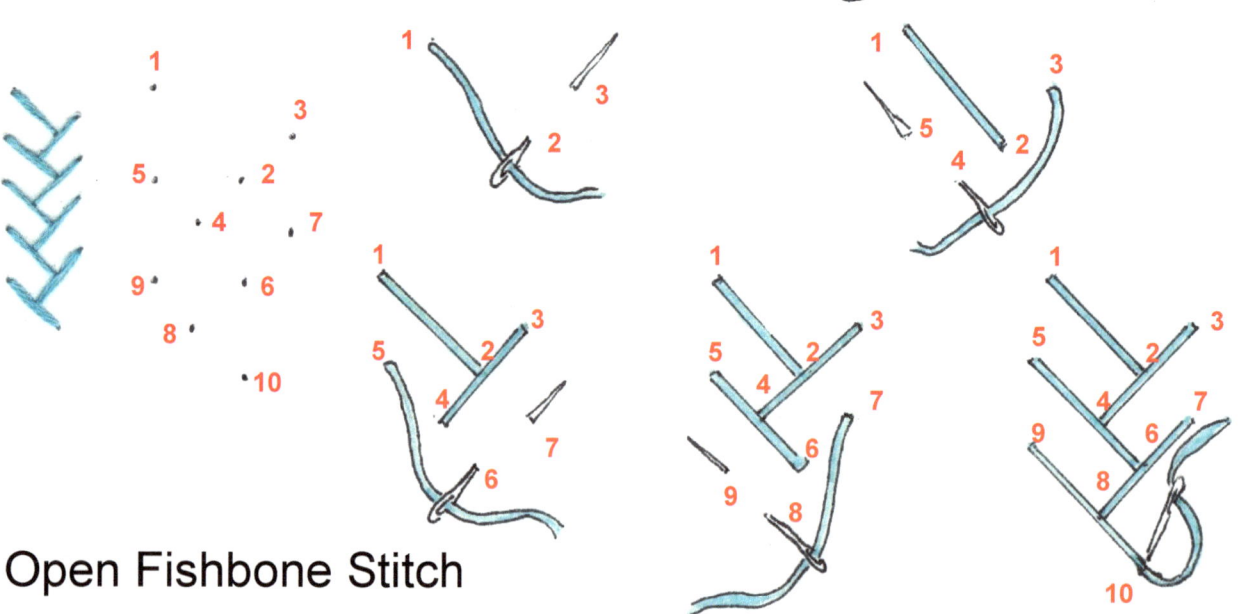

* All even numbers go in at the center

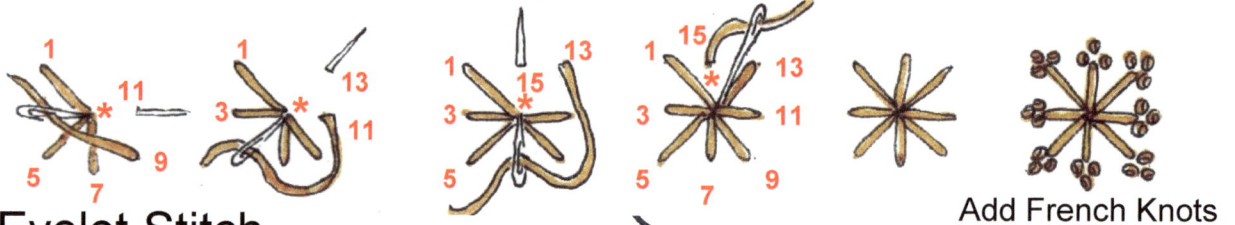

Add French Knots

French Knot

Open Fishbone Stitch

Straight Stitches

Straight

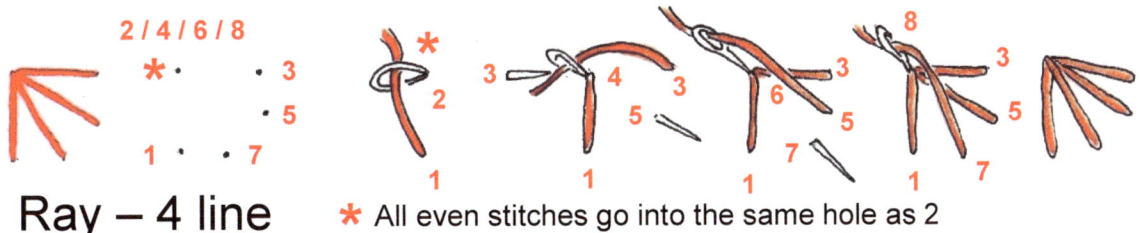

Ray – 4 line

✱ All even stitches go into the same hole as 2

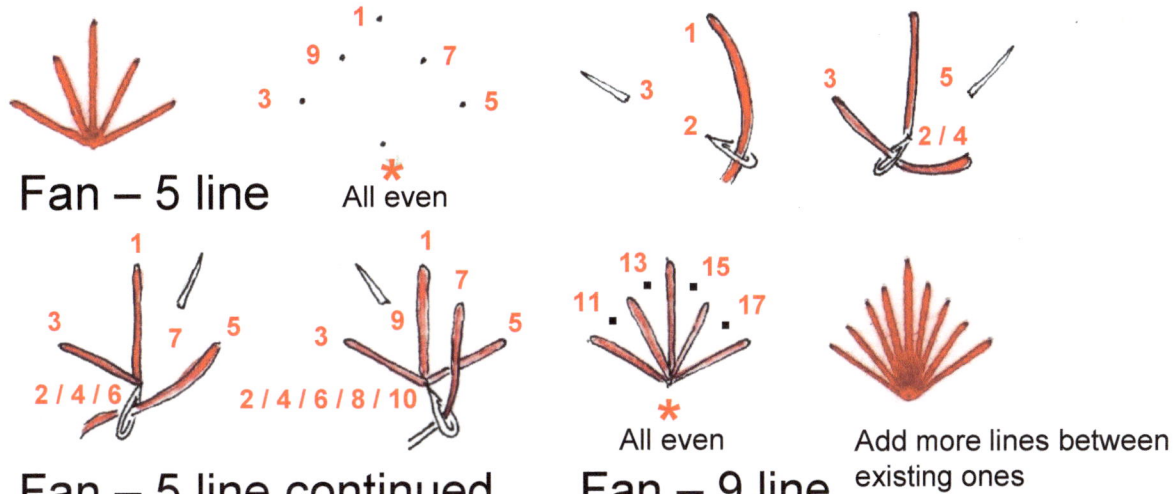

Fan – 5 line

✱ All even

Fan – 5 line continued   Fan – 9 line

✱ All even

Add more lines between existing ones

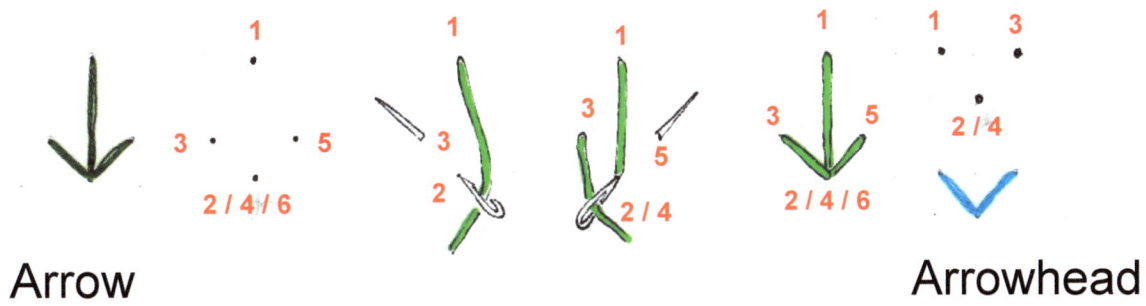

Arrow   Arrowhead

Trailing Stitch

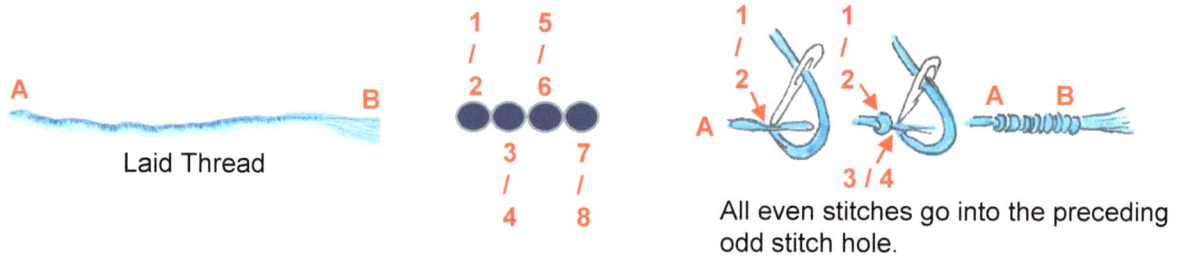

Laid Thread

All even stitches go into the preceding odd stitch hole.

A laid thread (A - B) is wrapped with the same color thread in another needle which comes up and goes down in the same hole for each stitch as shown by 1 / 2. The next stitch 3 / 4 is placed as close as possible to the preceding stitch without overlapping or crossing it. The new stitches completely cover the laid thread as they travel from A to B. The laid thread can be 6 to 12 strands of embroidery floss or a cord. In the examples below, the quilter used laid yarn.

The wheat motif has the trailing stitch in the kernels and on the leaf. The eagle has it on the sword and feathers.

From Farmer's Day Crazy Quilt

From OWB Crazy Quilt

Index of Stitches

Index of Stitches

Combinations

About the Author

Heather grew up in Oregon. Her introduction to sewing began while watching her mother and grandmother making a variety of projects for home and family. Formal lessons began in 5th grade "Home Ec." class and continued through high school. Following a break for university education and a career in teaching, including art, she returned to her love of sewing. She has served for several years as president of two quilt guilds, exhibited many prize winning quilts in shows and has taught numerous classes on quilting, machine embroidery and hand embroidery.

Heather currently lives in the Midwest and, with years of sewing traditional quilts, she is now exploring unusual quilts with 3-D patterns or unexpected embroidery stitches. An example is this one that starts out as a lazy daisy and ends up as a chained feather.

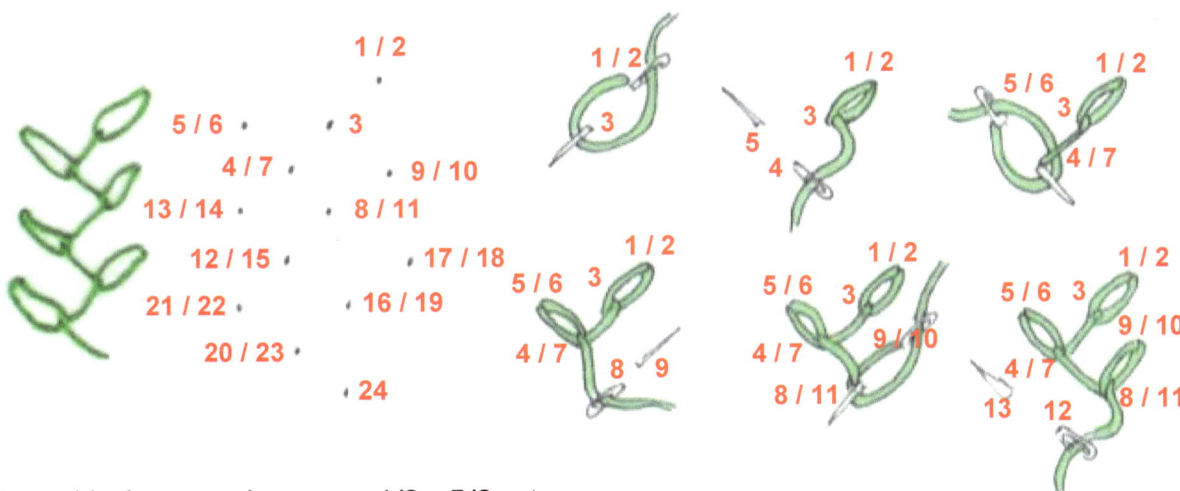

Shared holes are shown as 1/2, 5/6, etc.

Chained Feather

www.ingramcontent.com/pod-product-compliance
Lightning Source LLC
Chambersburg PA
CBHW061353090426
42739CB00002B/12